Poetry of Civilization

Poetry of Civilization

Mythopoeic Displacement in the Verse of Milton, Dryden, Pope, and Johnson

Sanford Budick

New Haven and London, Yale University Press, 1974

Designed by John O. C. McCrillis
and set in Baskerville type.
Printed in the United States of America by
The Vail-Ballou Press, Inc., Binghamton, N. Y.

Published in Great Britain, Europe, and Africa by
Yale University Press, Ltd., London.
Distributed in Latin America by Kaiman & Polon,
Inc., New York City; in Australasia and Southeast
Asia by John Wiley & Sons Australasia Pty. Ltd.,
Sydney; in India by UBS Publishers' Distributors Pvt.,
Ltd., Delhi; in Japan by John Weatherhill, Inc., Tokyo.

For Emily

Contents

Quod modo proposui, non est sententia: verum
    est,
credite me vobis folium recitare Sibyllae.

Juvenal

Preface

In 1944, some months before he died, Ernst Cassirer cast a final, backward glance at the incarnadine history of man's public mythmaking. Perhaps because of the nature of his subject, perhaps because of his inexpressible horror at the cataclysmic turn of recent events, Cassirer chose to conclude his last testament with a combination of parabolic myth and *applicatio:*

> Marduk, the highest god, . . . had to fight a dreadful combat. He had to vanquish and subjugate the serpent Tiamat and the other dragons of darkness. He slew Tiamat and bound the dragons. Out of the limbs of the monster Tiamat he formed the world and gave to it its shape and its order. . . . The world of human culture may be described in the words of this Babylonian legend. It could not arise until the darkness of myth was fought and overcome. But the mythical monsters were not entirely destroyed. They were used for the creation of a new universe, and they still survive in this universe. The powers of myth were checked and subdued by superior forces. As long as these forces, intellectual, ethical, and artistic, are in full strength, myth is tamed and subdued. But once they begin to lose their strength chaos is come again. Mythical thought then starts to rise anew and to pervade the whole of man's cultural and social life.[1]

The darkness of myth must be overcome, says Cassirer, but the substance of myth, subdued and transformed, provides at least

1. *The Myth of the State* (New Haven, 1969; first published 1946), pp. 297–98.

a large part of the substance of culture. The limbs of monstrous myth somehow become the body of culture.

There is, of course, a dramatic element of inner conflict in
Cassirer's view. Though he conceives of culture as deriving its
life from myths that can never wholly disappear, as a philosopher of Enlightenment he yearns for an amythic civilization.
Mythic thought is the enemy to be destroyed. For him the
great hero of culture in its battle against myth was Plato: "In
order to create the rational theory of the state, he had to lay
the ax to the tree: he had to break the power of myth." Plato,
we are told, was the champion of *logos* against *mythos,* dialectic against mythic imagination with all its productions of
art and poetry: "To admit poetry meant to admit myth, but
myth could not be admitted without frustrating all philosophic efforts and undermining the very foundations of Plato's
state." In "developing his political theories," says Cassirer,
"Plato became the professed enemy of myth. If we tolerate
myth in our political systems, he declared, all our hopes for a
reconstruction and reformation of our political and social life
are lost." [2] Thus, in spite of Cassirer's profound recognition of
the dependency of culture on myth, he strongly implies that
Plato's ideal world, and his own, would be a state without
myth.

There is, of course, a second way of viewing these matters.
Nietzsche, we recall, traced the demise of vigorous civilization
to the first Enlightenment, that of the Greeks, and there
pointed his violently accusatory finger at what he called "Socratism." [3] In mounting this attack, Nietzsche may very well
have been acting out what Walter Kaufmann has called a
"Brutus-crisis"—a tortured desire to kill the image he loved
so that he might resurrect its power in himself. But to poster-
ity his assault has seemed almost exclusively negative.[4] In the

2. Ibid., pp. 67–71, 72.

3. Friedrich Nietzsche, *The Birth of Tragedy and the Case of Wagner,*
trans. Walter Kaufmann (New York, 1967), pp. 82 ff.

4. *Nietzsche: Philosopher, Psychologist, Antichrist* (Princeton, 1968), p.
398. Kaufmann (p. 393) attempts to distinguish "Socrates" from "Socratism" in Nietzsche's thought. For a less sympathetic evaluation of Nietzsche's attacks on Socrates, see Crane Brinton, *Nietzsche* (Cambridge, Mass.,
1941), pp. 83–84.

onset of the Platonic malady Nietzsche saw the "philosophic thought" which "overgrows art and compels it to cling close to the trunk of dialectic." The long-term result, according to Nietzsche, is the "annihilation" of myth by dialectic, after which only "degenerate culture" remains.[5]

Nietzsche's and Cassirer's antithetical views intersect in the assumption that an essential tenet of Socratism and, by implication, of Enlightenment ideology was that the tree of mythos must be cut down and only the trunk of logos left standing. Whether we happen to count ourselves among those who, like Cassirer, glorify the mission of Socratism or who, like Nietzsche, revile it, there is apparently no dissenting from the view that Socratism and its spiritual heir, the Enlightenment, refuse to recognize that the work of Marduk should have any lasting relationship with Tiamat. And yet perhaps there is still another way of understanding the relation of logos to mythos—a relation in which creative coexistence is somehow imaginable. We may miss a vital part of Western man's heritage of mythmaking if we fail to see that there is, in fact, such a thing as the critical or dialectical use of myth.

Too many of us have become accustomed to thinking of Enlightenment thought and art as a foursquare structure reared on an adamantine epistemology: a *monumentum aere perennius* (such as Horace would make),[6] to be sure, but one whose resonance is only that of vast abandoned halls, somber precincts from which all living myth has been forever banished. We forget or try to explain away the fact that even at the height of their concern for dialectic, Socrates and Plato conspired to perpetuate many of the most influential myths in the tradition of Western civilization. We tend to disregard the continued existence, in the same tradition, of a strand of dialectically controlled mythmaking.

The principal aim of this study is to point to the leading features of this special mythmaking. After setting out the terms and limits of the subject, I will commence with Plato himself; for it was his ironic art and his dialectical operations upon myth that first exemplified what might be called the

5. *Birth of Tragedy*, pp. 91, 106, and 107.
6. *Carmina*, 3, 30, 1.

mythopoetics of displacement, the antimythic reversion to an antecedent myth. Horace and Juvenal, I will try to show, cultivated much the same public poetic. From them it was passed on, massively reinforced by analogous biblical paradigms and, perhaps most spectacularly, by Milton, to the English Augustan poets. These poets of the modern Enlightenment are my ultimate concern. The most striking feature of their generally remarkable ratiocinative activity will emerge as the way in which they supervised the perilous passage of myth into non-myth and of non-myth into resurrected myth.

In methodology my study is both macroscopic and microscopic. On the one hand, I have tried to keep at the center of attention what seem to me some of the largest and most exigent problems in creating or maintaining civilized thought. On the other, I have minutely examined the arguments of specific literary works. An enterprise of this kind is, I am aware, susceptible to the worst extremes both of high-flying pretentiousness and of groveling pedantry. If I have in some measure avoided either of these deadly sins, the credit belongs to the band of friends and counselors who have generously offered advice and encouragement. Frederick M. Ahl, James Hutton, and Michael C. Stokes of Cornell provided careful guidance in matters classical and philosophical. The manuscript as a whole was painstakingly read and improved by M. H. Abrams, Douglas N. Archibald, and Scott Elledge of Cornell; Ronald Paulson of Johns Hopkins; and Maynard Mack of Yale. At numerous points my text has benefited from the watchful eyes of Barbara Folsom and Merle Spiegel of Yale University Press.

For permission to reprint, in substantially revised form, materials which originally appeared in *ELH* (1970), I wish to thank the editors of that journal. An early version of my remarks on *The Dunciad* formed the core of a lecture delivered to a gracious audience of the Association of University Teachers of English in Israel. The lecture was subsequently printed in the *Proceedings* of the Association for 1971. Christopher Fynsk, my excellent student aide, took upon himself the largest part of the work of preparing the index. At crucial junctures my work was generously facilitated by grants from the American Philosophical Society and the American Council of Learned Societies.

This book is dedicated to my wife. Without her "sweet Converse and Love so dearly join'd," all my thoughts would long have fled to "wild Woods forlorn."

S.B.

Ithaca
Jerusalem, 1972

1

The Integration of Logos and Mythos

Poor Tom Taney, goldsmith and Ranter of the Strand, who in 1650 suddenly circumcized himself and announced quite simply, "I Proclaime from the Lord of Hosts," [1] is a grotesque symbol of his age's painful longing for a form of supernal authority. In the midst of chaotic groping of this kind—which did not significantly diminish in intensity for another hundred years—the major Augustans somehow succeeded, as Reuben Brower has said, in reaffirming "the public role of the poet, the Graeco-Roman conception of the poet as the voice of a society." [2] It is difficult to be specific about the nature of this role, perhaps because it is itself partly mythic. But what it meant to the Augustans may to some extent be gathered by glancing at a commonplace of literary history.

Unlike the labels of most literary ages, the adjective *Augustan* was not first applied by a later age. The term is preeminently self-descriptive. Dryden and Dr. Johnson, those two geniuses of age-labeling who seem to have enslaved us forever to the use of the name *metaphysicals,* stood at the boundaries of their own age and called it Augustan. Their preference for this term is implicit or explicit in many of their valuations of their own poetry. In the famous last sentences of the *Life of Dryden,* for example, Johnson draws on Suetonius's account of Augustus to say of Dryden that

1. Thomas Taney, *I Proclaime from the Lord of Hosts* (London, 1650).
2. *Alexander Pope: The Poetry of Allusion* (Oxford, 1959), p. 11. Brower's immediate reference is to Dryden's achievement.

> By him we were taught 'sapere et fari,' to think naturally
> and express forcibly . . . it may be perhaps maintained
> that he was the first who joined argument with poetry.
> . . . What was said of Rome, adorned by Augustus, may
> be applied by an easy metaphor to English poetry em-
> bellished by Dryden, "lateritiam invenit, marmoream re-
> liquit," he found it brick, and he left it marble.[3]

This is not merely graceful metaphor. Johnson, of course,
was careful to reinforce his own English bricks with Roman
supports, and in his praise of Dryden's writing there is an
implied relation between Dryden's place as the Augustus of
English literature and the ability "to think naturally," "express forcibly," and join "argument with poetry." What that
relationship might be, Johnson never makes clear. But Dryden,
too, apparently felt that it existed. It is fair to say, I think,
that the Augustan age in English poetry begins not so much
with the restoration of the Stuart line as with the imaginative
arrogation of the Augustan analogy to the poet's perception of
the English king. In the *Astraea Redux* (1660), Dryden's final
words of welcome are

> Oh Happy Age! Oh times like those alone
> By Fate reserv'd for Great *Augustus* Throne!
> When the joint growth of Armes and Arts foreshew
> The World a Monarch, and that Monarch *You.*[4]
>
> [ll. 320–23]

These lines invoke a world of special dependencies. The poet
of Augustan Rome was able to write because the emperor's
power provided a "Happy Age," while the emperor of Augustan Rome was able to rule, the poet suggests, because the
poet—in the person of Virgil or Horace—was able to assert
or "foreshew" the mythic a priori authority of the emperor.
It was necessarily a *"joint* growth of Armes and Arts" and

3. *Lives of the English Poets,* ed. George Birkbeck Hill (Oxford, 1905),
1 : 469.

4. Citations from Dryden's poetry are taken from *The Poems of John
Dryden,* ed. James Kinsley, 4 vols. (Oxford, 1958).

Dryden, clearly, thinks of himself as poet to Augustus. Twenty-five years later, Dryden's *Threnodia Augustalis,* his adieu to one Stuart and welcome to another, reasserts this special relationship:

> Live then thou great Encourager of Arts,
> Live ever in our Thankful Hearts.
>
> [ll. 383–84]

It is not true, of course, that the English Augustans were appealing exclusively to a Roman analogy of order and calm. As J. W. Johnson has shown, there is undoubtedly too much euphoria in Saintsbury's portrait of "the Peace of the Augustans." [5] Dryden was well aware that Augustan Rome was not an ideal world, for writers or anyone else. In his *Discourse concerning the Original and Progress of Satire* he observes that "Augustus, who was conscious to himself of so many crimes which he had committed, thought . . . to provide for his own reputation by making an edict against lampoons and satires." Dryden's ultimate preference for Juvenal over Horace is related to his feeling that the Augustan ideal is announced more clearly by the post-Augustan Juvenal than the technically Augustan Horace. In comparing the two poets he tells us that Juvenal's spirit

> has more of the commonwealth genius; he treats tyranny, and all the vices attending it, as they deserve, with the utmost rigour: and consequently, a noble soul is better pleased with a zealous vindicator of Roman liberty than with a temporizing poet, a well-mannered Court slave, and a man who is often afraid of laughing in the right place; who is ever decent, because he is naturally servile.[6]

5. James William Johnson, *The Formation of English Neo-Classical Thought* (Princeton, 1967), pp. 13 and 28. For another view of this subject see Howard Erskine-Hill, "Augustans on Augustanism: England, 1655–1759," *Renaissance and Modern Studies* 11 (1967) : 55–83.

6. *Of Dramatic Poesy and Other Essays,* ed. George Watson (London, 1962), 2 : 132–33. For remarks on the possible historical inaccuracy of Dryden's comments, see Niall Rudd, "Dryden on Horace and Juvenal," *University of Toronto Quarterly* 32 (1963) : 164–67. Pope and his contem-

It was the "real" Rome of Juvenal that helped furnish the
"Augusta" of Dryden's *Mac Flecknoe*. "Fair *Augusta* much to
fears inclin'd" (l. 65) is the antiworld of the true Augustan
ideal that Horace and Virgil tried to establish in their relationship with the throne.

We should also note that the positive vision indirectly suggested by the ironic portrait of Shadwell—the antitype of the
true poet—relies as much on comparisons with the authority
of a biblical-prophetic voice as with the ideal of Augustan poetry. Shadwell is a "mortal foe to Rome" (l. 113), as well as
the "last great Prophet of Tautology" (l. 30) for whom Flecknoe prepares the way (ll. 32–34), as St. John the Baptist did
for Christ. The closing image of the poem, which carries the
degeneration of the poetic ideal to what Dryden considered
the logical extreme, once again invokes the biblical voice as
the greatest possible contrast.

To advance any further in our delineation of the public
voice of the poet—of its authority and responsibility—we
must recognize, with Brower, that the role of spokesman for
a legitimate temporal or divine power itself derives from both
biblical and classical sources.[7] It was thus a traditional role
that was important to both major constituents of English Augustan culture; but modern accounts of it are not as available
as one would imagine. Perhaps the single most useful description of the elements constituting it appears in Gerhard Friedrich's history of the ancient herald, or *keryx*.[8] Friedrich notes
that an essential point about the heralds of classical and biblical society is that both political and religious significance
was attached to their proclamation (*kerygma*), but "the report
which they give . . . does not originate with them. Behind it
stands a higher power. The herald does not express his own
views. He is the spokesman for his master." Friedrich explains

poraries, in any case, maintained many of the views expressed by Dryden:
see *The Letters of Alexander Pope*, ed. George Sherburn (Oxford, 1956),
3 : 420, and Maynard Mack, *The Garden and the City: Retirement and
Politics in the Later Poetry of Pope, 1731–1743* (Toronto, 1969), p. 176.

7. *Alexander Pope*, p. 6.

8. *Theological Dictionary of the New Testament*, ed. Gerhard Kittel,
trans. Geoffrey W. Bromiley (Grand Rapids, Mich., 1965), 3 : 683–718.

that in Homeric society this master was the king; in the world of the Old Testament the prophets were described as the heralds of God; and in the person of Jesus, we are told, "the true preacher is God or Christ Himself." In the New Testament "the decisive thing is the action, the proclamation itself. . . . The divine intervention takes place through the proclamation." John the Baptist's "preaching of repentance is also prophecy," but Jesus "does not announce that something will happen. His proclamation is itself event. . . . The [*kerygma*] is the mode in which the divine Logos comes to us." [9]

Thus Friedrich points out that in both the classical and biblical traditions the role of the public spokesman came with more or less explicit powers and assumptions. These powers were also claimed by secular philosophers—in ways that remind us of the Cynic diatribe.[10] Epictetus, for example, "compares the Eleusinian [*keryx*] to the philosopher. . . . His proclamation is something sacral. . . . The peace [says Epictetus] which the philosopher proclaims is higher than that which the emperor can grant. . . . [The Stoic] declares, not the forgiveness of sins, but the development of the good. In place of the incarnation of God, he sets the divinisation of man." [11]

In recent years there has been a startling renascence of kerygmatic thought in the theological writings of Rudolf Bultmann and his followers. The larger outline of Bultmann's attempt to revive the proclamation implicit in New Testament mythology is interesting to us for what it indicates of the process that must precede proclamation and for what it tells us of the nature of the proclamation itself. He explains that the New Testament myths must be "demythologized" in such a way that the trappings of irrelevant mythology can be stripped away while the existential description of life represented by the configurations of the myth is revitalized as a new myth in the kerygma. Bultmann's theological opponents have argued

9. Ibid., pp. 688, 689, 696, 704, 706, and 716.

10. Cf. Gilbert Highet, *The Anatomy of Satire* (Princeton, 1962), pp. 24–66, as well as Highet's article "Satura" in *The Oxford Classical Dictionary*, ed. M. Cary et al. (Oxford, 1949).

11. *Theological Dictionary*, pp. 692–94.

convincingly that his approach is not really new.[12] But his account is still valuable as an explicit articulation of what was before only implicit, and for students of literature it is extremely useful as a hint of the procedures involved in the larger kerygmatic tradition, secular and religious.

For the truth is, I think, that the program Bultmann has suggested—of dismantling one myth *in order to* proclaim another—is used extensively in classical and biblical literature wherever a public voice is required to speak out on matters of public concern. Bultmann discusses supernatural mythology and a supernatural proclamation. The procedure he describes is equally applicable, I suspect, to any myth, defined simply as a communal assumption of obscure origin.

In considering imaginative literature we must be especially careful not to misunderstand the valency of the displacing process that Bultmann has called *de*mythological. Its significance is very far from being merely negative or destructive. Indeed, its meaning for the tradition of Western poetry is so much a living, growing thing, that it will be best to resist the temptation to base our discussion on any ready-made system of terminology. A particular choice of technical vocabulary will, in the end, matter far less than keeping at the fore the identifying features of our subject: the public voice speaking out on matters of public concern; the attempt to effect a seemingly antimythic extraction of myth; the enterprise of reviving a forgotten core of communal assumptions; the heroic straining of the civilized mind to glimpse the future through the species's recollected experience of the past. Ours must primarily be an inductive attempt to view more clearly the contours of an ongoing imaginative effort to create what Maynard Mack has recently called "the eternal City of man's recurring dream of the civilized community," a city in which "Vision should be united to Power, Wisdom—in the Socratic and Judaic sense—fructified in the fiats of statesman and chief." [13] Wisdom in the Socratic sense is our first order of inquiry.

12. See *Kerygma and Myth, A Theological Debate,* ed. Hans Werner Bartsch (New York, 1961).

13. *The Garden and the City,* pp. 3 and 212–13.

Plato's *Politicus*

Perhaps nowhere else in the Platonic canon is there better material for disproving Nietzsche's charges against Socratism, as well as for qualifying Cassirer's despairing admonitions, than in the mysterious, hyperrationalistic *Politicus*. This so-called critical dialogue has as its dual purpose the exposition of true dialectical method and the analytic isolation of the ideal statesman.[14] Here the maieutics of the master have already achieved independent life. Socrates himself issues the invitation to the dialogue and then withdraws to become an attentive onlooker until, at the close, he approves the work of the main speaker, the Eleatic Stranger, as done to perfection.

What strikes the reader immediately and repeatedly is the unyielding insistence on the long route of dialectical clarity. Not only must the searcher after truth be prepared to climb about and about the cragged and steep hill. He must also be ready to detour into what may seem like a distressing descent. The interlocutor, Young Socrates, constantly imagines that the Stranger's exposition must, at last, be at an end. Again and again he is forced to gather his philosophic courage for a new excursus whose justification does not strike him as being at all obvious. "Our chief purpose," the Stranger reminds him —holding out a crumb of bewildering comfort—is not to "find the Statesman" but to become "better philosophers, more able to tackle all questions": our "real subject" is the Statesman, but the subject is only of secondary importance; "what we must value first and foremost, above all else, is the philosophical method itself, and this consists in ability to divide according to real Forms" (285d–287a). More and more the Stranger seems preoccupied with the dialectic of finding true dialectic. Here indeed dialectic seems to overgrow everything around it.

But what is this hard-won dialectic of which the Stranger is so enamored? We learn that, from a technical standpoint, it is

14. See J. B. Skemp, ed. and trans., *Plato's* Statesman (London, 1952), pp. 13–14. All quotations from the *Politicus* in my text are from Skemp's translation.

the art of division according to true "cleavages" of reality
(259d ff.).[15] Only with this art can we distinguish the forms.
Only with the knowledge it affords can a ruler hope to order a
community in accordance with the real shape of the cosmos.
Mere politicians, for whom philosophy and statesmanship are
things apart, imagine that on the basis of superficial experience and cursory contemplation they thoroughly understand
the forms of life, and that they are adequately equipped to
install a communal Golden Age. Nothing, Plato's satiric ire
tells us, could be further from the truth. Such men, and the
constituencies that propagate and encourage their fancies, ig-
nore the need for precise and profound knowledge of even
the most vital matters. It is as though an edict should be issued announcing that the laws, say, of medicine and seamanship will be formulated on such and such a day by "men of
no calling or men of any other calling" with "the advice of a
few doctors and sailors maybe," that the laws so formulated
will be inscribed on "tablets of wood and of stone" and "some
of the rules so resolved upon" must "find their place among
the unwritten ancestral customs," that "thereafter for ever
medicine and navigation may only be practiced according to
these laws and customs," and that "if a man be found guilty of
enquiry into seamanship or medicine in contravention of this
law—of enquiry into nautical practice, for instance, . . . and
especially if he be guilty of airing theories of his own on such
things, action must be taken to suppress him" (298a–299b).
    Young Socrates's reaction to this brave new world is strangely
compelling. In it we hear an eerie echo (and prophecy) of the
most dramatic *responsum* of Socrates's career, his refusal to
yield to the Athenian authorities: "I cannot hold my peace
because that would be to disobey the god. . . . An unexam-
ined life is not worth living" (*Apology*, 37–38).[16] The reader's
imagination searches for the gay eyes, ancient and glittering,

15. For useful commentary on the varieties of Platonic dialectic, see
E. Kapp, *Greek Foundations of Traditional Logic* (New York, 1942), pp.
31–36.

16. Though the *Politicus* was written between 366 and 361 B.C., the
"dramatic date is 399, immediately before the trial and death of Socrates.
This dramatic date is remarkably well observed in so late a dialogue"
(Skemp, p. 23).

of Socrates's wraith as Young Socrates utters his full-bodied ab-
horrence (out of character, for him) of an embargo on research:
"the result would be that life, which is hard enough as it is,
would be quite impossible then and not to be endured" (299e).
The moment is climactic. From the reassertion of the Socratic
elenchus—the right, indeed the calling, to expose the incon-
sistency of what appears to be perfect logic but which is none-
theless false—emerges a cardinal point of the dialogue: the
exposure and correction of "rampant" error in the dialectical
description of reality in general and of political constitutions
in particular (297c). We gradually come to realize that the
rationalistic exposition of the Stranger from Elea has to do
more than a little with heeding a variety of hidden gods.

The rampant error to which the Stranger has immediate
reference is the illusion men nourish that present-day political
constitutions are close on the heels of godlike perfection. For
reasons deeply rooted in their mythic assumptions, men believe that an arrangement of man-made laws can produce an
earthly paradise. The Stranger explains that all the manifold
codes men invent are only pathetic attempts to chase "the fading vision of the true constitution," which men once glimpsed
but which they no longer recall (301e). In order to deny the
mythological axioms that lie behind contemporary political
theory, the Stranger carefully prepares his own mythological
major proposition. In the end we must not be shocked to find
that the conclusion of the dialectic is itself mythic.

Although the dialectician's use of myth seems a self-contra-
diction and even a sharp falling-off from philosophical dignity, Plato chooses to introduce a "massive myth" to impugn
the veracity of contemporary political mythifying and to differentiate sharply between gods and those unfeathered bipeds
(266e) called men. All at once the dialectical march is halted
and the entire company is invited to gambol among the lotus
of legend. "We have to bring in some pleasant stories," the
Stranger offhandedly announces, "to relieve the strain":

> There is a mass of ancient legend a large part of which
> we must now use for our purposes; after that we must go
> on as before, dividing always and choosing one part only,

until we arrive at the summit of our climb and the object of our journey. [268d]

With hindsight, we know before the fact that the myth is offered in a form which is somehow incomplete: soon after finishing his narrative the Stranger will say, "we reared our massive myth and then had to use more myth-material than the occasion warranted; thus our demonstration became too long and we did not give the myth a complete form after all" (277b). The myth is massive and complex and mysterious. But it is in itself fascinating and, ultimately, it is of the greatest significance for Plato's argument as a whole: [17]

There is an era in which God himself assists the universe on its way and guides it by imparting its rotation to it. There is also an era in which He releases His control. He does this when its circuits under His guidance have completed the due limit of the time thereto appointed. Thereafter it begins to revolve in the contrary sense under its own impulse—for it is a living creature and has been endowed with reason by Him who framed it in the beginning. . . .

This change of motion we must regard as the most important and the most complete of all 'turnings back' occurring in the celestial orbits. . . . At the time such changes take place in the Universe we human beings living within that universe have to undergo the most drastic changes also. . . . In the cosmic crisis there is widespread destruction of living creatures other than man and . . . only a remnant of the human race survives. Many strange new experiences befall this remnant. . . . Every living creature . . . ceased [18] to grow any older. . . . A new race

17. For general discussions of the myth, see (besides Skemp's admirable introduction) J. A. Stewart, *The Myths of Plato* (London, 1905), pp. 173 ff., P. Frutiger, *Les Mythes de Platon* (Paris, 1930), pp. 241–49, and P. M. Schuhl, *La Fabulation Platonicienne* (Paris, 1947), pp. 89–104.

18. Constant shifting of tense may itself be a mysterious aspect of the myth of reversal.

[was] formed from men dead and long laid in earth but now formed in her womb anew and thence returning to life once more. Such resurrection of the dead was in keeping with the cosmic change, all creation being now turned in the reverse direction. . . . All good things come without man's labour [in] the former era. . . . A god was their Shepherd and had charge of them and fed them even as men now have charge of . . . creatures inferior to them —for men are closer to the divine than they. When God was Shepherd there were no political constitutions. . . . Men rose up anew into life out of the earth, having no memory of the former things. Instead they had fruits without stint from trees and bushes; these needed no cultivation but sprang up of themselves out of the ground without man's toil. . . . This is the story, Socrates, of the life of men under the government of Kronos. Our present life . . . you are alive to experience for yourself.

. . . When this whole order of things [i.e., the first era] had come to its destined end, there must needs be universal change once more. For the earth-born seed had by now become quite exhausted. . . . And now the Pilot of the ship of the Universe (for so we may speak of it) let go the handle of its rudder and retired to His conning-tower in a place apart. . . . A shudder passed through the world at the reversing of its rotation, checked as it was between the old control and the new impulse which had turned end into beginning for it and beginning into end. . . . At first [the world] remembered His instructions more clearly, but as time went on its recollection grew dim. . . . And [as] forgetfulness of God arises in it, the ancient condition of chaos also begins to assert its sway. . . .

The God looks upon it again, He who first set it in order. Beholding it in its troubles, and anxious for it lest it sink racked by storms and confusion, and be dissolved again in the bottomless abyss of Unlikeness, He takes control of the helm once more. . . .

This is the full tale told, but to meet our need—the

delineation of the king—it is enough if we take up the earlier part of our tale. When the most recent cosmic crisis occurred and the cosmic order now existing was established, the course of man's life stood still once more and then began to manifest changes in the opposite sense to the changes accompanying the other cosmic crisis. . . . It has now been ordained that the Universe must take sole responsibility and control of its course. . . . Thus likened to the Universe and following its destiny through all time, our life and our begetting are now on this wise now on that.

Here let our work of story-telling come to its end, but now we must use the story to discern the extent of the mistake we made in our earlier argument in our delineation of the King or Statesman. [269c–274d]

Here, finally, the myth draws to a close and is made to merge explicitly with the dialectic. One more distinction or division can now be made clear. Prematurely, we begin to emit bated breath when we hear that the "massive myth" enables us to see that we go wrong when we take from the first

cosmic era the Shepherd of the human flock as it then was, and [describe] him as the statesman. He is a god, not a mortal. . . . The Divine Shepherd is so exalted a figure that no king can be said to attain to his eminence. Those who rule these states of ours in this present era are like their subjects, far closer to them in training and in nurture than ever shepherd could be to flock. [274d–275c]

This, then, is the moral of the story. But is this all? we ask. Were we given so much myth for so little point—and an "incomplete" myth at that? The whole proceeding seems strange indeed.

And it remains so until we begin to understand that by reviving in man's primordial memory the "fading vision of the true constitution" which abides, as it were, in a collective unconscious, the Stranger offers to reestablish the epistemological connection between dialectic and the City in men's minds. The art of dividing according to the true cleavages of reality emulates the "divine ordering of the world," which "portioned out" human life in a divine government that itself obviated mere written constitutions; to "become better philosophers" is to find the Statesman; shoddy dialectic and tawdry imitative visions of a paradisal constitution necessarily go hand in hand. An ideally ordered city, we find, is thus a composite reflection of all the true forms relating to human existence. True reasoning is itself a myth-retrieving activity.

But all these implicit propositions fall far short of describing an efficacious mechanism for restoring substantiality to the genuine constitution—the true image of civilization. They are themselves incomplete discursive counterparts of the incomplete myth. Something is missing—not only in these propositions or in the myth itself, but also in the justification for the entire excursion.

In order to find this elusive quantity we must examine carefully the point at which the dialogue turns from dialectic to myth. There, we recall, the Stranger casually enforced a subtle distinction between one kind of story and another. The "story" (274d) or linked "stories" (268d) that he has introduced are to do more than "relieve the strain" of the inquiry: they are to displace other "old stories" which are embedded deep in men's assumptions but which falsify a true picture of reality by imitating it inaccurately:

> All these [inaccurate] stories originate from the same event in cosmic history. . . . However, as this great event took place so long ago, some of them have faded from man's memory; others survive but they have become scattered and have come to be told in a way which obscures their real connection with one another. No one has related the great event of history which gives the setting of all of them; it is this event which we must now recount. Once it has been related, its relevance to our present demonstration of the nature of a King will become apparent. [269b–c]

We have seen that this event (or series of events), which somehow cannot be related in complete form, seems to have only a misty relevance to the Stranger's argument. Knowledge of it compels us to see that we have falsely exalted the king by attaching to him aspects of the divine. The intuition or half-knowledge that prompted us to do this was itself not false. Men do possess an authentic perception of a divine political antecedent. But they are at present abused by several injurious notions. Our earthly kings, we must see, are decidedly secular; they run with the pack; they are fully accredited members of the herd. And our present-day constitutions are in no sense divine or paradisal or utopian. How then, one asks again, can we possibly make our way back to the anterior myth? The answer is complex and paratactic. It depends upon our comprehending the specialized syntax that governs the coexistence of dialectic and myth. It is a syntax in which subordinating connectives are fragile and vital in the highest degrees.

The Stranger's myth and dialectic have one feature clearly in common: both aim at disabuse of mistaken conceptions that are mythically rooted. This feature is obvious in the myth and in the part of the dialectic that exists as commentary upon the myth. We must also remember that the language of the dialogue's argument as a whole is on many occasions curiously mythic. Some politicians, the Stranger tells us, "are like lions, some like centaurs, or similar monsters. A great many are satyrs or chameleons, beasts that are masters of quick change in order to conceal their weakness" (291b). Much later we hear that this same "fantastic pageant that seemed like some strange masque of centaurs or some band of satyrs stands revealed for what it is. At much pains we have succeeded at last in distinguishing them [i.e. politicians] and setting them apart, as we must, from all true practice of Statesmanship" (303c–d). A true "vision" of the genuine constitution or leader emerges from the dismantling of existing myth and a *return* through the salvageable materials of that myth to an earlier myth. Indeed, from the point of view of the dialogue's larger strategy, the myth of recurrence and infolding is itself of no more than coequal importance with the presentation of the myth as an ironic or demythological reversal of traditional mythological materials, materials which themselves already contain the core of the poet's myth. In following this procedure, the Stranger reenacts the mysterious pattern of *reversal* which controls his massive *ur*-myth. He remedies man's "forgetfulness of God" which, we saw, brought with it "the ancient condition of chaos." The myth of the king is dead! he proclaims. Long live the myth of the philosopher-statesman!

The half-turn from divine to secular that is effected by combining myth and dialectic, issues in no mere dialectical statement; or rather it issues in a dialectic that we have been taught to regard as both a record of divine order and a blueprint for reapproach to the divine. We are not surprised to see that the dialogue ultimately comes full circle and culminates in a series of dialectical assertions which are themselves myths. This constitutes the long-awaited completion of the "massive myth," a completion which could only have come from the marriage of myth and dialectic. We learned before that the Divine Shepherd "is a god, not a mortal"; he is "so exalted a figure that no king can be said to attain to his eminence." Now, as the pageant of centaurs and satyrs is "revealed for what it is," the Stranger affirms that the rule of the philosopher-statesman "must always be exalted, like a god among mortals, above all other constitutions" (303b).

That which we too easily regarded as the dialectician's pastime yields divine refreshment. Unawares, we have scaled and crossed the Alps. We see now that the movement from divine to secular that graphs the tragic history of our era is reversible —and by human agency. The philosopher-statesman who orders the lives of his subjects in accordance with true dialectic also has the power to unite "that element in their souls which is supernatural by a divine bond, since this element in them is akin to the divine. After this supernatural link will come the natural bond, human ties to supplement the divine ones" (309c). By "the wondrous inspiration of the kingly art," the true Statesman is enabled to forge a "bond of true conviction" uniting, especially, "the hearts of the young folk." It is a kind of dialectical covenant to which the Statesman leads back his people after showing them that this divine truth abides in all men always, though they distort it and misapprehend it. He helps it to arise "in the soul of men" as "a right opinion con-

cerning what is good, just and profitable and what is the opposite of these—an opinion based on absolute truth and set-
tled as an unshakable conviction." This conviction the Stranger
declares to be "a manifestation of the divine occurring in a
race which is in truth of supernatural lineage." The philosopher-statesman has the miraculous power—"the talisman appointed . . . by the design of pure intelligence"—to reverse
the course of civilization's degeneration (309c–310a).

The myth is complete, the vision has been restored. But
where, we ask—as the dialogue itself fades away—is the philosopher-statesman to be found? Throughout the dialogue an
undercurrent of dramatic tension is generated by the suggestion that we are in fact listening to the philosopher-statesman
or that, perhaps, he is a certain onlooker. In the process of
becoming a better philosopher, the Stranger seems to have
found the Statesman—a man who is "just as much a king
when he is not in power as when he is" (293a). Yet Plato, recently escaped from serving as advisor to Dionysius of Sicily,
was apparently unwilling to suggest the practical means for
turning the academic philosopher into acting philosopher-
statesman. Although it seems clear that the exalted office would
have to be filled by a man who could combine the functions of
dialectician, mythographer, rhetorician, and administrator, the
Stranger systematically disqualifies such synthetic vocations as
prophet or herald—at least in the minimal terms in which
Plato conceived of these positions. Special status is, we find,
reserved for the orator who is not called, as are the prophet
and herald, the true king's "opposite" (261a); his office is sin-
gled out as "that department of the art of public speaking
which is closely allied to the kingly art" (304a).[19]

Plato's attitude toward rhetoric underwent successive revi-
sions as he moved from the *Gorgias* to the *Phaedrus* and then

19. Plato's austerely minimal definition of the herald as a robotlike
functionary is not totally relevant to our discussion since what is of interest to us is the expanding, creative role of the appointed spokesman—
the heraldic orator of the king, or the prophet sent by God—whose un-
deniable identity is poured into a sanctified mold of antiseptically depersonalized, established authority. Plato's orator is himself, in these
terms, the Statesman's herald.

to the *Politicus,* where the orator's position becomes tempt-
ingly vague. Here the orator seems to be a combination of
subordinate dialectical philosopher, qualified advisor almost as
competent as the king himself, and government spokesman.[20]
In his power to persuade "men to do what is right" (304a), the
orator even seems to share the Statesman's divine talisman. We
may think that we hear disparagement in the statement that
the orator has "the task of persuading the general mass of the
population by telling them suitable stories rather than by giving them formal instruction" (304c–304d), but there is nothing
to say that the orator cannot enrich his tales with instruction
for more discriminating palates. Indeed, we cannot forget that
on this very occasion the Stranger from Elea has been careful
to offer us a combination of dialectic and pleasant story—as
do so many of the Socratic dialogues, whether or not they deal
with the Statesman. We cannot forget that it was only by this
means that the Stranger from Elea was able, in his own terms,
to subdue a satyr and reveal a god.

20. See Skemp, pp. 218–19 n.

2

The Heraldic Voice: Horace, Juvenal, Jeremiah

Dryden was only translating from Dacier—who was paraphrasing Casaubon, who was echoing Rabelais and Erasmus, who were themselves rehearsing a familiar *topos* in the history of satire—when he compared the *Sermones* of Horace to the mysterious Silenus Alcibiadis:

> I cannot give a more just idea of the two books of satires made by Horace than by comparing them to the statues of the Sileni, to which Alcibiades compares Socrates in the *Symposium*. They were figures which had nothing of agreeable, nothing of beauty, on their outside; but when any one took the pains to open them, and search into them, he there found the figures of all the deities.[1]

The ancient simile is extremely happy. It reminds us subtly yet powerfully of the Socratic refusal to disobey the god within and it recalls endless, laborious attempts to bring forth that god through the art of maieutics, or dialectical midwifery. The figure combines the audacious irreverence of the inebriate satyr with his strange power to speak divine truth. And it symbolizes the amalgam of piercing rationality and supernal mythmaking that is so important a part of the Socratic achievement. The application of the simile to Horace's satires implies that the same qualities are to be found in Horace and, per-

1. *Of Dramatic Poesy and Other Essays,* ed. George Watson (London, 1962), 2 : 140. See W. P. Ker, ed., *Essays of John Dryden* (Oxford, 1900), 2 : 285 and, especially, Erasmus, *Opera Omnia* (Leiden, 1703), 2 : 770 ff.

haps, in all satire; and it also implies a relation, in Dryden's mind at least, between Socrates and Horace.

Horace

Without reference to Dryden or Dacier, scholars have recently shown renewed interest in the Socratic elements in Horace's satires. Eduard Fraenkel has noted that, in book 2 in particular, Horace departed significantly from Lucilian satire by employing the Socratic dialogic form, and that some of Horace's introductory sentences are even "meant to recall passages in famous dialogues of Plato." [2] In a compelling essay, W. S. Anderson has argued further that "Horace modelled his satiric mask on Socrates" and the Socratic writings, and that in so doing he followed his own explicit advice: "rem tibi Socraticae poterunt ostendere chartae [your matter the Socratic pages can set forth]" (*De Arte Poetica*, 310). Horace, Anderson explains, declared his independence of denunciatory Lucilian satire, which relied heavily on the tradition of the Cynic-Stoic diatribe. The diatribe ("an approximate Greek equivalent of the Latin *sermo*") "owed its origin to Socrates and the Socratic writers." Horace went "back beyond Lucilius and the Cynic-Stoics to Socrates himself for his model." Horace's "ridentem dicere verum" (telling the truth with a laugh), often cited as the apotheosis of his satire, itself "summarizes the methods of Socratic irony": "the poetic genius" of book 2 "lies in its Platonic features." There the reader is "expected to do precisely what Plato asks of his readers, to criticize the foolish speaker with [his] own rational faculties and thus to reach a clearer comprehension of the moral truth than the speaker possesses." In book 2 the "chief character," the satirist's interlocutor, is "a teacher who fails to grasp the implications of his own precepts and thus ends as a figure of fun." [3]

Anderson's study makes it easier for us to see that the rational discourse of Horace's satires, like that of Socratic maieu-

2. *Horace* (Oxford, 1957), p. 136.

3. "The Roman Socrates: Horace and his Satires," in *Satire: Critical Essays on Roman Literature,* ed. J. P. Sullivan (Bloomington, Ind., 1968), pp. 1–37.

tics, is a kind of Silenic drama in which matters of the highest
import are broached to the understanding through the seemingly destructive medium of satiric irony. But by overstating
Horace's rejection of Lucilius, Anderson has, I think, deprived
himself of the opportunity of gathering one of the choicest
fruits of his exposition. If we turn to *Sat.* 2.1, for example—
a satire which was to have a decisive influence in molding the
satiric stances of Persius and Juvenal, Dryden and Pope—we
find that the polemic against Lucilius, upon which Anderson
so much insists, itself becomes a way of offering signal praise
to Lucilius and of turning him into a myth of the satirist's
place and power.

In this satire, we recall, Trebatius is asked for legal advice
concerning the "lawful bounds" of satire (ll. 1–2).[4] Much of
the power of the composition derives from the gradual revel-
ation that the true subject is not so much legality as the nature of Horace's art and its relation to the structure of the
state. Trebatius's reply to the poet's vexed plea for counsel
is simply "Quiescas [Take a rest]" (l. 5). But this the poet
cannot do. It would be to disobey his inner voice: "I cannot
sleep," "write I must" (ll. 7, 60). Horace's assertion of demon-
like compulsion follows immediately an offhand reference to
"deadly hemlock" (l. 56). It is hard to imagine that Horace
did not plant this phrase to reinforce the suggestive analogy
between Socrates's appearance before the Athenian bar to de-
fend his vocation, and Horace's pleading with C. Trebatius
Testa in defense of his calling. Horace's answer in these lines
sounds like a careful evocation of Socrates's refusal, in the
Apology, to abandon his elenchus. Horace writes:

> whether peaceful age awaits me, or Death hovers round
> with sable wings, rich or poor, in Rome, or, if chance
> so bid, in exile, whatever the colour of my life, write I
> must. [ll. 57–60]

The Socratism of the satire extends far beyond dramatic
analogy; or, to put it another way, the dramatic analogy sub-

4. All quotations from Horace are from *Horace: Satires, Epistles and
Ars Poetica,* trans. H. Rushton Fairclough (Cambridge, Mass., 1966).

serves a larger Socratic design. Trebatius, the "figure of fun" who speaks more truth than he knows, provides the seeds of a meaningful artistic solution to Horace's problem even while he tenders mere cynical legalism:

> If such a passion for writing carries you away, bravely tell of the feats of Caesar, the unvanquished. Many a re- ward for your pains will you gain. . . . You might write of himself, at once just and valiant, as wise Lucilius did of Scipio. . . . How much wiser this than with bitter verse to wound . . . whereupon everybody is afraid for himself, though untouched, and hates you. [ll. 10–23]

Judged by contemporary conceptions of what satire has been, the configuration of poetry, politics, and morality that Treba- tius sketches is not monstrous: the poet sits at the feet of power, where he offers incense and mildly espouses ethical and social principles; for this Caesar smiles and rewards him amply. Common knowledge had it that Horace had already been asked to set a dainty dish of epic song before Caesar. Why not comply? In doing so Horace would be fulfilling the office of the emperor's poet—or would he?

Horace's own descriptions of Lucilius in the fourth and tenth satires of book 1 had not helped to settle the question. There he had managed to imply that Lucilius was ill-man- nered and overzealous in his pursuit of public virtue. The obverse of this early censure implied, in fact, a portrait of the true satirist very similar to that of the court dependent offered by Trebatius. Trebatius's fortunate "mistake" in iden- tifying Lucilius as a genial, time-serving poet gives Horace one more chance to revise his attitude toward Lucilius—and toward satire—and to discover in him the archetype of satiric virtue. Fraenkel has pointed out that Horace's readers would have sensed the self-consciousness of his change in attitude and that they would even have recognized in Trebatius's ad- vice, "bravely tell of the feats of Caesar," a direct allusion to similar venal advice that Lucilius had been given—and that he had spurned.[5]

5. Fraenkel, *Horace,* pp. 148–50.

Trebatius's tawdry views turn out to be golden at the core. Lucilius, Horace realizes, should be his model; indeed he has been carrying Lucilius's image within him all this while without realizing it. In defense of his calling he is early moved to say that his "own delight is to shut up words in feet, as did Lucilius" (ll. 28–29). In seeming opposition to Trebatius's penchant, Horace lauds Lucilius as one who

> first dared to compose poems after this kind [i.e. fearless satires] and to strip off the skin with which each strutted all bedecked before the eyes of men, though foul within. . . . He laid hold upon the leaders of the people, and upon the people in their tribes, kindly in fact only to Virtue and her friends. [ll. 62–70]

"Sequor hunc," Horace realizes more and more—"He it is I follow" (l. 34). His own mysterious origins cast him in the same poetic mold of defender of his country's integrity. Although the suggestion is clothed in humorous garb, we must strip off its satyr outside:

> I, a Lucanian or Apulian, I know not which, for the settlers in Venusia plough close to the borders of both lands. Thither they were sent, as the old story goes, when the Samnites were driven out, and to this end, that no foe might ever assail the Romans through an open frontier.
> [ll. 34–37]

"Quo ne per vacuum Romano incurreret hostes." The vacuum implied is clearly moral, spiritual, and poetic, though it is just as dangerous as any gaping defense-line.

Thus the structure of the satire depends on two parallel rehabilitations: one of Horace's image of Lucilius and one of the world's conception of weak-kneed satire. The ultimate meaning of the satire issues from the confluence of these two processes in Horace's reincarnation of an Age of Kronos—a Lucilian ideal of coexistence of poet and statesman that has abided all along in Trebatius's legalism and in Horace's recovery from his Brutus-like impulse toward Lucilius. Lucilius and the virtuous Romans who were his friends—those very friends referred to by Trebatius—make it possible for the satirist's art to embody a true heroism. "Wise Lucilius" could sing the praises of Scipio and yet remain "kindly in fact only to Virtue and her friends," merciless to all who deserved the sword of satire, because Scipio was both virtuous and Lucilius's friend. With Lucilius "virtuous Scipio and the wise and gentle Laelius withdrew into privacy from the throng and theatre of life . . . and flinging off restraint would indulge with him in sport while their dish of herbs was on the boil" (ll. 71–74). Lucilius was fortunate enough to find a way to take the virtuous kernel of the advice equivalent to that given Horace, "Caesaris invicti res dicere."

Fraenkel has remarked that

> a wide gulf was fixed between Lucilius, a senator's brother, himself a Roman knight, the intimate friend of Scipio and other great noblemen, and Horace, a freedman's son, who . . . after a narrow escape from the catastrophe of his patrons, had to pick his steps most carefully.[6]

And yet, without seeking to rise on the social scale, Horace has confirmed Trebatius's latent suggestion that the existence of a moral and an effective satire depends upon the free and independent association of the satirist with a virtuous center of political power. It is not without reason that, in the punning jest which closes the satire, Horace should modestly indicate to his readers that Caesar does indeed approve his satires. The "old story" of the satirist as preserver of the state —imperfectly babbled by Trebatius, awkwardly jested about by the poet—has been made new.

The implications of the first satire of book 2 of the *Satires* are further explored and more amply set forth in the first epistle of book 2 of the *Epistles,* the well-known "To Augustus." The epistle and the satire are symmetrical in much more than placement in their respective groups—as Horace surely recognized and fully intended. In the interval between the

6. Ibid., p. 80.

Satires and the *Epistles* the pressure upon him to "tell the feats of Caesar" had continued undiminished.[7] A central, recognizable feature of both *Sat.* 2.1 and *Ep.* 2.1 is, accordingly, the delicate *recusatio* in which Horace informs Augustus that he is really not capable of epic description. Both passages are mysteriously ironic in that both explicitly testify to Horace's substantial abilities in the use of this very idiom:

> neque enim quivis horrentia pilis
> agmina nec fracta pereuntis cuspide Gallos
> aut labentis equo describat volnera Parthi.

[Not everyone can paint ranks bristling with lances, or Gauls falling with spearheads shattered, or wounded Parthian slipping from his horse.]

[*Sat.* 2. 1. 13–15]

> nec sermones ego mallem
> repentis per humum quam res componere gestas,
> terrarumque situs et flumina dicere, et arces
> montibus impositas et barbara regna, tuisque
> auspiciis totum confecta duella per orbem,
> claustraque custodem pacis cohibentia Ianum,
> et formidatam Parthis te principe Romam,
> si quantum cuperem possem quoque.

[And for myself, I should not prefer my "chats," that crawl along the ground, to the story of great exploits, the tale of distant lands and rivers, of forts on mountain tops, of barbaric realms, of the ending of wars under your auspices throughout the world, of bars that close on Janus, guardian of peace, and of that Rome who under your sway has become a terror to Parthians—if only I had power equal to my longing.]

[*Ep.* 2. 1. 250–57]

The reason for the poet's incapacity to multiply verses in this vein is by no means self-evident. In the epistle, as before in

7. Cf. ibid., pp. 353 ff.

the satire, the explanation depends upon the reader's and/or Augustus's appreciation of the strong suggestion that the writer of such "chats" or *sermones* (a term Horace uses to describe both his *Satires* and *Epistles*) must be allowed to have a position that is both independent of Caesar and yet interwoven in Caesar's heroic charge.

This suggestion, which is, in my view, a large part of the raison d'être of the epistle, is methodically yet subtly developed throughout the piece. The epistle's closing *recusatio* is anticipated near the beginning of the poem, when Horace obliquely observes that epic, mythlike praise is not, in itself, necessarily a service to a great man:

> Romulus, father Liber, Pollux and Castor, who, after mighty deeds, were welcomed into the temples of the gods, so long as they had care for earth and human kind, settling fierce wars, assigning lands, and founding towns, lamented that the goodwill hoped for matched not their deserts. He who crushed the fell Hydra and laid low with fated toil the monsters of story found that Envy is quelled only by death that comes at last. For a man scorches with his brilliance who outweighs merits lowlier than his own, yet he, too, will win affection when his light is quenched. Upon you, however, while still among us, we . . . set up altars to swear by in your name, and confess that nought like you will hereafter arise or has arisen ere now. [ll. 5–17]

The passage is complex. In it we find much of sincere compliment: Horace unhesitatingly links Augustus with the most revered names in Roman history and story.[8] But we also find the suggestion that at least some of the praise that has been proffered to Augustus is rather overdone: no one, after all, can know now who will "hereafter arise," and some of the figures mentioned even in these few lines (like Romulus and Hercules) make us wonder if there is any point to the ranking superlatives of Augustus's encomiasts. What remains of the minuend, after unfair neglect has been lamented and hy-

8. Cf. ibid., p. 385.

perbolic eulogy has been delicately censured, is the "goodwill" that merit deserves—a concept which is held in suspension until we approach the end of the poem, where we hear, " 'tis worth inquiring what manner of ministrants attend on Merit, tried at home and in the field" (ll. 229–31).

In the meantime Horace embarks on a lengthy disquisition (ll. 18–213) intended, as Fraenkel says, to clear away "the prejudices of the reactionary critics and the general reader" so that the new poetry Horace stands for can be allotted "its proper place in the body politic." When the long-delayed inquiry is finally taken up, we realize that Horace's bulldozer has not bothered to spare even a few of the emperor's pet ruins, especially the ancient Roman comedies Augustus caused to be frequently performed.[9] This bold even-handedness is more than constancy to an ideal of critical objectivity. It implies that the poet, as critic of literature and of society, has his appointed work which cannot be neglected and which declares his dignity and the regard of even the emperor. We become aware that much that is said in the poem is controlled by an initial irony—one meant not to rend and deracinate but to revise and extend. The opening lines subtly overstated Augustus's sole responsibility for the many departments of Roman life:

> Seeing that you alone [solus] carry the weight of so many great charges, guarding our Italian state with arms, gracing her with morals, and reforming her with laws, I should sin against the public weal if with long talk, O Caesar, I were to delay your busy hours.

As one of the ministrants on merit—a "Virtus" which comes to be equated with Augustus[10]—the poet participates in the emperor's excellence by acknowledging it, pruning it, and extending it into all activities of the state. The emperor must have heralds, and these must be men who are much more than yea-saying lackeys. Horace points out that it is "to the giver's great renown" that

9. Ibid., pp. 388 and 396.
10. Ibid., p. 396.

> Virgil and Varius, those poets whom you love, discredit
> not your judgment of them nor the gifts which . . . they
> have received; and features are seen with no more truth,
> when moulded in statues of bronze, than are the manners
> and minds of famous heroes, when set forth in the poet's
> work. [ll. 245–50]

The emperor is dependent on such poets. His generosity to
them shows his discernment, and it is only through them that
his subtlest achievements—his mind and manners—can be
made an organic part of Rome's life. Horatius Flaccus, a herald of another kind, also serves, though his ministry is of a
different type. He is the herald tried at home, as Virgil and
Varius are those of the field:

> Though a poor soldier, and slow in the field, he serves
> the State, if you grant that even by small things are great
> ends helped. The poet fashions the tender, lisping lips
> of childhood; even then he turns the ear from unseemly
> words; presently, too, he moulds the heart by kindly pre-
> cepts, correcting roughness and envy and anger. [ll. 124–
> 29]

The poet, who carries about him the never-fading memory of
"Romulus, father Liber, Pollux and Castor," has been dele-
gated the crucial tasks of educating and adjusting human abilities, especially of the young. It is this office which makes him
the indispensable counterpart of the emperor-statesman. Augustus could not manage alone; indeed, he should not wish
to. Horace's recusatio—his epiclike declination to write epic
or myth—has become the sublimated basis for his creation of
another kind of epos, the reviving of a flesh-and-blood trans-
migration of a departed image. Lucilian goodwill has made
his sermones vital to the public weal. His works fulfill a special kind of epic charge by enlarging the emperor's heroic
merit in poems that are not "sheets of useless paper," but
"volumes" to match, improve, and communicate Augustus's
conceptions of what is worthy of Apollo and his temple (cf.
ll. 216–18 and 264–70).

Juvenal

We are not surprised to find that Juvenal's program for satire, in various ways the spiritual and literary inheritor of Horace's,[11] also relies on a return to a Lucilian myth of pristine power and inescapable vocation:

> I will tell you why I prefer to run in the same course over which the great nursling of Aurunca [Lucilius] drove his horses. [*Sat.* 1. 19–21]

> It is hard *not* to write satire. [l. 30]

> Must I not deem these things worthy of the Venusian's [Horace's] lamp? [l. 51]

> Who can get sleep . . . ? Though nature say me nay, indignation will prompt my verse. [ll. 77–79]

> Lucilius roars and rages. [ll. 165–66] [12]

Though we do not find in Juvenal a marked indebtedness to a Socratic mask, the myth-retrieving outlines of his procedure are in fact more clearly drawn than those of Horace. Martial's influence on Juvenal was perhaps crucial here.[13] G. G. Ramsay explained fifty years ago that

> Juvenal and Martial may . . . be said to have developed a school of practical poetry. Just as Socrates is said to have called down the attention of men from the heavens to the earth, so did Juvenal and Martial call men from the barren repetition of mythological tales and fancies . . . to describing the life of men as lived in their own time and city.[14]

---

11. For a discussion of this relationship see E. J. Kenney, "The First Satire of Juvenal," *Proceedings of the Cambridge Philosophical Society*, n.s. 8 (1962) : 36 ff.

12. All quotations from Juvenal are from *Juvenal and Persius*, trans. G. G. Ramsay (Cambridge, Mass., 1965; first published 1918).

13. For comment on the relation of Martial to Juvenal see, especially, R. E. Colton, "Juvenal and Martial" (Ph.D. diss., Columbia University, 1951).

14. Ramsay, ed., *Juvenal and Persius*, p. xlix.

The comparison with Socrates is inevitable; for Socratism is deeply rooted (as we noted earlier) in the same Cynic tradition from which both Martial and Juvenal, as well as Lucilius and Horace, sprung. But we have seen that the Socratic use of myth is often deceptively dismissive and that, in fact, the restoration of a refurbished myth can be one of the central aims of Socratic dialectic. The same aim, or one very like it, belongs to the voice of Juvenal, declaiming for the salvation of Rome in Satire 1. Gilbert Highet points out that this satire

> contains a fundamental distinction which runs all through Juvenal's work. . . . Most literature, [Juvenal] says, is superfluous, because it has nothing to do with real life. Most poetry is merely long-winded reconstruction of Greek myths, of stories which were often pretty silly in themselves and have now been so hackneyed that they are revolting. . . . Juvenal . . . holds that the only kind of literature which has any genuine reason for being written —*now*, in his own day—is satire. Satire deals with real life.[15]

Highet's account is valuable but lacking, I think, in the same ways that flawed Ramsay's sketch: Juvenal is not merely rejecting the old myths; and it is simplistic to speak of his satire as dealing with "real life." [16] Juvenal begins, it is true, with an excoriation of contemporary mythic modes, of all kinds. "What?" he asks, "Am I to be a listener only all my days? . . . Shall I have no revenge on one who has taken up the whole day with . . . an Orestes, which, after filling the margin at the top of the roll and the back as well, hasn't even yet come to an end? No one knows . . . so well as I . . . from what country another worthy is carrying off that stolen golden fleece."

Juvenal does not simply discard these myths, however. "If you can give me time," he says, "I will tell you why I prefer" to follow the example of Lucilius (ll. 20–21). The reasons his discursive faculty discovers are not simply threats to the

15. *Juvenal the Satirist* (New York, 1961), p. 48.
16. See Kenney, "First Satire of Juvenal," p. 37, on this point.

Roman ideal of living. They are, I suspect, satiric counterparts or contemporary equivalents of the vaunted mythologies.
Some of these are now obscure, but Juvenal's design is clear
enough. Instead of an Oresteian tragedy we have a man who
is "thrust on one side by men who earn legacies by nightly
performances, and are raised to heaven by that now royal
road to high preferment—the favours of an aged and wealthy
woman" (ll. 37–39). Instead of Jason and his argonauts we
have "the people hustled by a mob of retainers attending on
one who has defrauded and debauched his ward" (ll. 46–47).
Juvenal does violence to these myths not simply to destroy
them, but to pull out their hearts, to release their essences.
"Should I do better," he asks further on, "to tell tales about
. . . the lad who splashed into the sea?" No, he says, just look
around you: "See the youngster dashing at break-neck speed
. . . holding the reins himself, while he shows himself off to
his great-coated mistress" (ll. 52–62). But Juvenal cannot help
asking (through his imaginary interlocutor), where will I get
the freedom to name names as contemporary vice requires? If
I libel the great they'll burn me alive (cf. ll. 155–57).

His answer, which is also the conclusion of the poem, is
not, I believe, abrupt and unsatisfying, as Highet feels. Juvenal labors to extend and to make powerfully explicit that
criticism of the heroic ideal which Virgil had registered only
implicitly. In a recusatio that has powerful affinities with Horace's and was to become a mainspring of sublimated energy in
the counterheroic tradition, Juvenal tells us that he will not
regress to an old myth and "set Aeneas and [King Turnus]
a-fighting with an easy mind" (ll. 162–63). Instead he will em-
ploy the energies and heroic assumptions underlying such a
myth to cast a new myth and to become its heraldic embodi-
ment. Like Lucilius, he will roar and rage "as if with sword in
hand" so that the hearer, "whose soul is cold with crime," will
grow red and sweat "with the secret consciousness of sin."

This will be his new mythology of "wrath and tears." The
heraldic "trumpet," he tells us, is about to sound (ll. 165–68).
The "fictive war," to use Maynard Mack's phrase,[17] is about
to begin. Villains who are already in the grave, he says, will

17. "The Muse of Satire," *The Yale Review* 41 (1951) : 92.

serve his purpose (cf. ll. 170–71)—perhaps even better than live ones, we may add, because they provide an element of mythic distance without being removed beyond lifelike familiarity. There is an important element of the nonreal in Juvenal's satire of "real life." It is the "fictionality" [18] of new-forged myths heated by the smoldering ashes of the old. Rome's wild career into degeneracy and chaos *can* be arrested. Rome may yet find her way back to an image of order and virtue.

Lest we begin to imagine that what I have been describing as poetry of civilization, exemplified by a poem like Juvenal's first satire, is merely reactionary longing for an aristocratic status quo, we must pass quickly to Juvenal's eighth satire, his systematic mortar-and-pestle pounding of hereditary "nobility." Although we have already met some of this satire's arguments in Satire 1, here we find heightened irreverence with a purposeful vengeance:

> What avail your pedigrees? What boots it, Ponticus, to be valued for one's ancient blood, and to display the painted visages of one's forefathers—an Aemilianus [the younger Scipio] standing in his car; a half-crumbled Curius; a Corvinus who has lost a shoulder, or a Galba that has neither ear nor nose? [ll. 1–5]

The question is not merely rhetorical. Once we have grasped the inner design of the satire we realize that, although pedigrees undoubtedly do count for nothing, visages of heroic forefathers—an individual's or a people's—may matter a great deal if they can be resurrected and made to live in thought and action. Within its seeming destructiveness, the poem relies heavily on images of retrieved mythic grandeur, which reemerge, fresh and alive, from the shattering of false embodiments of myth. Juvenal's special rehearsal of genealogy insures an artifactual survival of the myth in its original configuration:

> Why should a Fabius, born in the home of Hercules, take pride in . . . the Great Altar [of Hercules] if, as a traf-

18. Ibid., p. 84.

ficker in poison, he dishonour his unhappy race by a statue that will have to be broken in pieces? Though you deck your hall from end to end with ancient waxen images, Virtue is the one and only true nobility. [ll. 13–20]

The pretense of the Fabii to descent from Hercules is patently absurd. After all, the earliest Roman ancestor was either a rustic unknown or a criminal (cf. ll. 272–75). Only Virtue, fixed in a matrix of Herculean myth, is a standard of real value. Idols of false mythic affiliation with excellence are pulverized by the poet's anger or made molten by his contempt. The divine image has already been hacked to pieces and scattered to the winds by false gods, forces of the night; but a new Apis is waiting to be reconstituted and brought to life: "if you have proved yourself," Juvenal tells Ponticus, "to a rejoicing country a rare and illustrious citizen, we would fain cry what Egypt shouts when Osiris has been found" (ll. 27–30). Much the same remnant of configuration is traced in the demolition of the aristocratic "Cecropid, the image of a limbless Hermes": Juvenal sees the heroic profile reemerging in the plebian "brave young soldier who marches to the Euphrates, or to the eagles that guard the conquered Batavians." "In no respect but one," Juvenal tells the Cecropid, "have you the advantage over him: his head is of marble, while yours is a living effigy!" (ll. 51–55).[19]

What characterizes Juvenal's eighth satire, we see, is not its antimythic but its myth-revising or myth-reviving program. When Juvenal says, "What if I can never cite any example so foul and shameful that there is not something worse behind?" (ll. 183–84), he is not merely indicating the plentitude of vice; he is suggesting that behind everything vicious there stands a

19. The lines remind us of Ruskin's reconstructive advice to the burghers of Bradford, who invited him to instruct them in building an Exchange—an "idol of riches": "if you can fix some conception of a true human state of life to be striven for—life, good for all men, as for yourselves . . . you will build with stone well, but with flesh better; temples not made with hands, but riveted of hearts; and that kind of marble, crimson-veined, is indeed eternal." "Traffic," lecture 2 of *The Crown of Wild Olive.*

prototypical vice, an image of anti-virtue, which someone is always striving to reproduce. In recognition of this fact, Juvenal is unwilling to let lie the sleeping dogs of myth, whatever form they take: "the nimble Lentulus acted famously the part of Laureolus [a criminal]: deserving, in my judgment, to be really and truly crucified" (ll. 187–88).

By the same token, Juvenal suggests (even in his most offhand manner), it is the incandescent filament of myth which illuminates men's perceptions of their roles in relation to vice and virtue. This subtle but insistent suggestion is what gives substance and force to what Highet has called the "core" of the poem,[20] Juvenal's serious advice to Ponticus on his conduct as governor:

> If your whole staff be incorruptible: if no long-haired Ganymede sells your judgments; . . . if, in your circuit through all the towns and districts, there is no Harpy ready to pounce with crooked talons upon gold,—then you may trace back your race to Picus; [21] if you delight in lofty names, you may count the whole array of Titans, and Prometheus himself, among your ancestors, and select for yourself a great-grandfather from whatever myth you please. [ll. 127–34]

This kind of "supernatural lineage" (as the Eleatic Stranger would say)—the correlative of divine conviction—is closely associated with the talisman of the statesman and, we must add, of the statesman's counselor and herald, the educating poet. The surface paradox of the eighth satire is that nobility does not necessarily have anything to do with "nobility," that noble principles and actions are not the same as noble birth. But we must also recognize a deeper irony and distinction at work: the mythic grandeur which, in common conception, adheres to noble birth, belongs not to the nobleman but to the myths— the gold-misted images of glorious deeds that make the ancestor noble. In detaching this heroic essential from what has

20. *Juvenal the Satirist*, p. 113.
21. "A mythical Latin king, son of Saturn, and father of Faunus" (Ramsay's note).

become, in fact and act, nonmythic, and assigning it a proper place in contemporary reality, the heraldic satirist prosecutes his great design.

His tool must itself be a form of myth, for nothing else could loose the titanic hold of time-worshiped dispositions, as we see in the following passages, which together form the climax of the composition:

> If free suffrage were granted to the people, who would be so abandoned as not to prefer Seneca to Nero . . .? [Nero's] crime was like that of Agamemnon's son; but the case was not the same, seeing that Orestes, at the bidding of the Gods, was avenging a father slain in his cups. Orestes never stained himself with Electra's blood, or with that of his Spartan wife; he never mixed poison-drafts for his own kin; he never sang upon the stage, he never wrote an Epic upon Troy! For all the deeds of Nero's cruel and bloody tyranny, which was there that more deserved to be avenged by the arms of . . . a Galba? . . .
>
> Where then can be found, O Catiline, nobler ancestors than thine, or than thine, Cethegus? Yet you plot a night attack, you prepare to give our houses and temples to the flames. . . . But our Consul is awake, and beats back your hosts. Born at Arpinum, of ignoble blood, a municipal knight new to Rome, he . . . is alert on every hill. . . . Rome was yet free when she styled Cicero the Parent and Father of his country! [ll. 211–44]

Juvenal's program reaches fulfillment in the completion of the mythic vision. The image of a Galba that was before without ear or nose (perhaps like a syphilitic descendant), as Hermes was without limbs, is now seen to take up arms (*armis*) against the contemporary monster of vice who is more primitive and archetypal than ancient myth. In Nero there is no human conflict; he is the enemy of man's greatest moral myths, of his conglomerate epic vision. Why, indeed, should Juvenal bother with an *Orestes* or a ranting Theseid when he is surrounded by such living serpents? The old myths have not died, but they have changed bodies. Catiline and Cethegus, who are now one with the forces of night, have been displaced from the Roman tree of freedom and virtue. Their disinheritance makes room, in our imaginations, for Cicero, a new descendant of their ancestors, who becomes, in the ultimate extension of myth displacement, "the Parent and Father of his country." In the welter of myth and history, virtuous freedom enables the mind to witness the surfacing of the orator-heralds, the preservers and transmitters of Rome's civilized greatness. Among these, figures like Seneca or Cicero stand out tragically or triumphantly.

Still another figure, a moral writer like them, begins to lift his bowed head as the poem winds to its conclusion. "It is difficult," Highet justly remarks of this passage, "not to feel that Juvenal is thinking of his own merits, long ignored and now perhaps recognized for the first time. Like Cicero he was 'a knight from a little town': he was a patriot too, and he thought much of saving the state." [22] With Ponticus, the embryonic statesman, we, the poet's ultimate objects, have now been made to realize that without the massive myth, reflected and refracted by the strewn fragments of story, pointed and suggestively reassembled by the mosaicist of imagination, there would be no surviving glory. But now the mind has hurtled back to the great event which is the blaze at the origin point of all fading visions. This is the archaeological voyage of recovery to which our spirited guide referred when he advertised, "credite me vobis folium recitare Sibyllae"—"you may take it that I am reading out to you one of the Sibyl's leaves" (l. 126).[23]

Jeremiah

J. D. Duff asked, "was Juvenal a hero like the Hebrew prophets, who rebuked wicked kings to their faces?" [24] Histo-

---

22. *Juvenal the Satirist*, p. 115.

23. For a different interpretation of these lines see A. M. Kurfess, "Juvenal und die Sibylle," *Historisches Jahrbuch* 76 (1957) : 79–83.

24. J. D. Duff, ed., *D. Ivnii Ivvenalis Satvrae XIV*, with a new introduction by Michael Coffey (Cambridge, 1970; first published 1898), p. xxxiv.

rians have not yet answered the question with certainty. For
our purpose it is enough to say that Dryden, the father of Augustan verse satire, was convinced the answer was yes. In fact,
the influence of Juvenal in Dryden's poetry (and in Pope's)
tends to merge with that of the great biblical writers. There
were certainly enough similarities in method to engender an
easy blending of satire and jeremiad in the Augustan mind. If
we take the third chapter of Jeremiah himself, for example,
we find a procedure which is remarkably close to that of Juvenal. As we recall, the chapter opens with Jeremiah's attack
on the regression of the Israelites to naturalistic, hedonistic
idolatry:

> 1 They say, If a man put away his wife, and she go from
>   him, and become another man's, shall he return unto
>   her again? shall not that land be greatly polluted?
>   but thou hast played the harlot with many lovers; yet
>   return again to me, saith the Lord.
> 2 Lift up thine eyes unto the high places, and see where
>   thou has not been lien with. . . .
> 6 The Lord said . . . unto me in the days of Josiah the
>   king, Hast thou seen *that* which backsliding Israel
>   hath done? she is gone up upon every high mountain
>   and under every green tree, and there hath played the
>   harlot.[25]

The prophet employs a sexual analogy because it describes
the spiritual infidelity of Israel in forceful terms and because
it is a real account of one part of their idolatrous immorality
(cf. 5 : 7–8). But these descriptions of transgression are subordinate to the prophet's larger goal: to renew the covenant of
the land, the land which expresses the unique relationship
between God and the people of Israel. It is for this reason
that the idolatry and the sexuality are formulated in terms of
abuses of the mountains and trees: "she is gone up upon every
high mountain and under every green tree." The act of demythology takes place at the moment when the naturalistic

25. The translation is that of the King James Version.

perversion of the holiness of the land—in idolatry and adultery—is exposed:

> 9 And it came to pass through the lightness of her whoredom, that she defiled the land, and committed adultery with stones and with stocks.

Once reason has shattered the supernaturalistic façade that conceals mere idolatry, the proclamation can be heard. Jeremiah's main effort is then to reassert the mythic value of the land as a symbol of the true relationship between Israel and the divine:

> 11 And the Lord said unto me, . . .
>
> 12 Go and proclaim these words toward the north, and say, Return, thou backsliding Israel, saith the Lord. . . .
>
> 13 Only acknowledge thine iniquity, that thou hast transgressed against the Lord thy God, and hast scattered thy ways to the strangers under every green tree. . . .
>
> 14 Turn, O backsliding children, saith the Lord; for I am married unto you. . . .
>
> 15 And I will give you pastors according to mine heart, which shall feed you with knowledge and understanding.
>
> 16 And it shall come to pass, when ye be multiplied and increased in the land. . . .
>
> 17 At that time they shall call Jerusalem the throne of the Lord; and all the nations shall be gathered unto it, to the name of the Lord, to Jerusalem: neither shall they walk any more after the imagination of their evil heart.
>
> 18 . . . and they shall come together out of the land of the north to the land that I have given for an inheritance unto your fathers.

The voice that speaks here is both the prophet's and God's. The prophet or herald of God is maximally defined. He is no unthinking functionary. He is, as A. J. Heschel has said, "a

participant, as it were, in the council of God, not a bearer
of dispatches whose function is limited to being sent on er-
rands. He is a counselor as well as a messenger. . . . As a
witness, the prophet is more than a messenger. As a messenger, his task is to deliver the word; as a witness, he must
bear testimony that the word is divine." [26] The proclamation of the poet fulfills itself when he gives voice to the acknowledgment that was required to purify and reestablish
the mythic relationship between people and God—again in
terms of the land, a return to the true God of the land:

> 21   A voice was heard upon the high places, weeping *and*
>   supplications of the children of Israel: . . .
>
> 22   . . . Behold, we come unto thee; for thou *art* the
>   Lord our God.
>
> 23   Truly in vain *is salvation hoped for* from the hills,
>   *and from* the multitude of mountains: truly in the
>   Lord our God *is* the salvation of Israel.

Finally, in verse 25, there is an ultimate acknowledgment of
the proclamation, of "the voice of the Lord our God." Jeremiah tells us in chapter 1, that God set him "over the nations
and over the kingdoms, to root out, and to pull down, and to
destroy, and to throw down, to build, and to plant" (1. 10). We
see that it is in demythology and proclamation that this
charge is fulfilled.

Jeremiah's destroying and building constitute one continuous imaginative act which has become crucial in the Judaeo-
Christian tradition. It is, at its best, a massive effort to make
new the old coherence by rescuing it from a distorting incrus-
tation of idolatry and hypocrisy. Jeremiah's categorical statement of this process (in chapter 31—it is repeated almost
verbatim by St. Paul in Hebrews 8 : 8–10) is as follows:

> 31   Behold, the days come, saith the Lord, that I will
>   make a new covenant with the house of Israel, and
>   with the house of Judah:
>
> 32   Not according to the covenant that I made with their

26. *The Prophets* (New York, 1962), pp. 21–22.

fathers in the day *that* I took them by the hand to
bring them out of the land of Egypt; which my covenant they brake, although I was an husband unto
them, saith the Lord:

33 But this *shall be* the covenant that I will make with
the house of Israel; After those days, saith the Lord,
I will put my law in their inward parts, and write it
in their hearts; and will be their God, and they shall
be my people.

In his commentary on this passage, Calvin eloquently rendered Protestant understanding of Jeremiah's prophetic con-
tinuum:

Now, as to the *new* covenant, it is not so called, because
it is contrary to the first covenant; for God is never in-
consistent with himself, nor is he unlike himself. He then
who once made a covenant with his chosen people, had
not changed his purpose, as though he had forgotten his
faithfulness. . . . Whence do we derive our hope of salvation, except from that blessed seed promised to Abraham? . . . Why are we called the children of Abraham,
except on account of the common bond of faith? Why
are the faithful said to be gathered into the bosom of
Abraham? Why does Christ say, that some will come from
the east and the west, and sit down in the kingdom of
heaven with Abraham, Isaac, and Jacob? (Luke xvi. 22;
Matt. viii. 11.). . . . God has never made any other covenant than that which he made formerly with Abraham,
and at length confirmed by the hand of Moses. . . . The
covenant which God made at first is perpetual.
    . . . The substance remains the same. By substance I
understand the doctrine; for God in the Gospel brings
forward nothing but what the Law contains. We hence
see that God has so spoken from the beginning, that he
has not changed, no not a syllable, with regard to the
substance of the doctrine. For he has included in the Law
the rule of a perfect life, and has also shewn what is the
way of salvation, and by types and figures led the people

to Christ, so that the remission of sin is there clearly made manifest, and whatever is necessary to be known. . . . It was . . . in some respects, a new thing, that God regenerated the faithful by his Spirit, so that it became not only a doctrine as to the letter, but also efficacious, which not only strikes the ear, but penetrates into the heart, and really forms us for the service of God.[27]

Despite upheaval, the continuity is unbroken. Indeed, it is only because of prophetic and imaginative violence that the covenantal seed can be transmitted intact and renascent.

27. *Commentaries on the Book of the Prophet Jeremiah and the Lamentations,* trans. John Owen (Edinburgh, 1854), 4 : 126–30.

3

Milton's Epic Reclamations

If it is true that in reaffirming the public role of the poet the Augustans did what, according to Brower, Milton "could not do," [1] it is also true, I believe, that the Augustans, in large measure, were able to succeed because of what Milton had done. He offered them a model for the supremacy of logos over mythos, of reason over Satanic idol-making, and in specific cases he provided them with a foundation myth of Marduk's victory over the serpent Tiamat. The truth of these statements must be substantiated in some detail.

Though the periodicity of Milton's career may seem to suggest a segregation of public, discursive involvement from private, poetic detachment, we must remind ourselves that Milton himself resisted any such distinction. Aside from the massive, general contemporaneity of his "Restoration" *Paradise Lost,* poem after poem, early and late, in Milton's poetic corpus bears witness to the fact that his imagination was fired by the events and issues of his age. This is not to say that Milton ever shows much interest in what is usually called journalistic verse—even in the best senses of that term. As a poet, he chose to skirt history. For him the medium of enduring verse could not be dependent on the exigencies of the moment. But Milton was too much immersed in the Hebrew prophets and in the classics to evade—or, indeed, wish to evade—the contemporary referents of his poetic consciousness. Milton self-consciously chose for himself the role of prophet to the English nation—he believed the charge had been thrust upon

1. *Alexander Pope: The Poetry of Allusion* (Oxford, 1959), p. 11.

him—and his poetic works reveal in varying degrees his
abiding aspiration to renew a divine covenant and to proclaim
timeless truths of special contemporary public significance. A
discussion of three works—the sonnet "On the Late Massacre
in Piemont," *Samson Agonistes,* and *Paradise Lost*—will, I
hope, help to define Milton's "Prophetic strain" [2] and to lay
the foundation for considering his influence upon the mythmaking of Augustan verse.

"On the Late Massacre in Piemont"

On 24 April 1655 a shock wave was sent through the Protestant world by the massacre of the Vaudois, a mysterious, cen-
turies-old community of pre-Reformation Protestants. Roman
Catholic soldiers, acting under more or less direct orders from
the duke of Savoy, were soon known to be the perpetrators.
For Commonwealth England, insecure in its own violent equilibrium of papal and antipapal passions, and hardly recovered
from fratricidal wounds, the shock was especially severe. Cromwell himself led a public relief campaign and directed his sec-
retary of foreign tongues, Mr. Milton, to send appropriate
protests and calls for aid to Denmark, France, Savoy, Sweden,
the Swiss cantons, and the United Provinces.[3]

Milton was powerfully moved by the event. Even the moder-
ated official responses of his "left hand" (the instrument, Milton said, of his prose endeavors) [4] bespeak a mind fervently
engaged. In letters of high discursive tension, Milton outlines
the relevant issues of religious toleration, freedom of minor-
ities, and the responsibility of governments to insure the safety

2. *Il Penseroso,* l. 174. All citations from Milton's poetry are to *John
Milton: Complete Poems and Major Prose,* ed. Merritt Y. Hughes (New
York, 1957).

3. For commentary on the sonnet, see: *The Sonnets of John Milton,* ed.
Mark Pattison (London, 1883); *The Sonnets of Milton,* ed. John S. Smart
(Glasgow, 1921); *Milton's Sonnets,* ed. E. A. J. Honigmann (London,
1966); and Kester Svendsen, "Milton's Sonnet on the Massacre in Pied-
mont," *Shakespeare Association Bulletin* 20 (1945) : 147–55.

4. *Complete Prose Works of John Milton,* ed. Don M. Wolfe et al.,
5 vols. (New Haven, 1953–71), 1 : 808. All citations from Milton's prose
are to this edition.

of individuals. Except for a few flashing moments, rhetorical passion is largely absent. But in those few moments the nature of Milton's imaginative stake becomes clear. For all the political and religious urgency of the hour, Milton yearned to abstract the Vaudois from temporality and to see them detached as "the eldest practicers of the orthodox religion . . . the most ancient root of a purer religion"—"remnants of primitive believers" who were forced to wander "over the wildest mountains and through perpetual winter." [5] Their plight, like their faith, was undateable, eternal. The tragic event was part of the divine plan and the divine promise. In verse Milton fulfilled the promise of his perception. With his poetic right hand, he composed his mind and his soul in a sonnet that has often been called the greatest in the English language.

The datum of catastrophe became a tunnel to the past. Milton saw in the massacre an opportunity for re-creating the past in the present and of superimposing one on the other. In the letter to the United Provinces, Milton spoke tentatively of the Vaudois as "men among whom our religion was handed down from the very first doctors of the Gospels and was preserved uncorrupted, or else was restored to its pristine wholeness long before it was among other nations." [6] When he sat down to write the sonnet, his imagination seized tenaciously on the first possibility and converted it to certainty: the martyrs *were* the faithful remnant who kept God's "truth so pure of old / When all our Fathers worship't Stocks and Stones." The ten-horned monster who persecuted the Lord's faithful is still holding sway as the "triple Tyrant." Once this temporal reversibility is established, the door of historical imagination flies open and we find ourselves standing, not with Sir Samuel Morland in seventeenth-century Savoy, where the bones of Vaudois "Lie scatter'd on the *Alpine* mountains cold," but with Jeremiah and John in the biblical Holy Land. We stand with a martyred faithful remnant who kept God's "truth so pure of old / When *all our Fathers*"—not Druids or

5. Ibid., 5 : ii, 836–37, and 688. The first letter quoted was written three years after the massacre.
6. Ibid., ii, 693. Milton retained drafts of all three letters cited here.

Etruscans but the entire unbelieving biblical world—"committed adultery," in Jeremiah's phrase, with Stocks and Stones. The poet's "Ev'n them" is not merely intensive, it is stereoscopically inclusive and additive. In the stark, stabilizing phrase "Forget not," the desperate oscillations of historical multiconsciousness are brought under control. Thereafter a regular weaving of past and present ensues.

The sonnet, thus analyzed, is seen to consist of choric incantations. Additional strophes describing the present ("in thy book . . . Rocks"; "Their martyr'd blood . . . Tyrant") are succeeded by additional antistrophes from the biblical past ("Their moans . . . Heav'n"; "that from these . . . *Babylonian* woe"). Words and phrases that straddle both moments— "thy book," "Mother with Infant," "Vales," "triple Tyrant," "*Babylonian* woe"—help form the reader's perception of the ceaseless recapitulation of providential pattern. Behind the parallelism, mysterious forces of fateful echo and reenactment push the sonnet toward a vision of regeneration. The defiled mountainsides, littered with dry bones, witness a quickening spirit. After being described as massacred in their "Fold" in the fiftieth word of the sonnet, the Vaudois are themselves "redoubl'd"—made to live again in the hundredth word, "hunderd-fold" (original spelling). In the mystical patterning of pain and providence the "triple Tyrant" has caused God's saints triple moans: "Their moans / The Vales redoubl'd to the Hills, and they / To Heav'n."

Here, as in Yeats's *Second Coming,* there is turning and turning in the gyre. But here the center does hold. Here the ceremony of innocence is submerged again and again, but it is not drowned because in the fusion of past and present the poet is enabled to proclaim the future—a promise of ultimate, stable redemption. From the sonnet's fabric of Old Testament, New Testament, and classical regeneration myths, symbolic of Christian man's entire mythic experience, emerges a prayer for sanctified renewal which is also a prophecy of continued holy life. The repetition of the past atrocity in the present has been made warrant for proclaiming the repetition in the present of past redemption and of past prophetic foreshadowing of universal salvation.

Milton's sonnet is punctuated by a series of hierophantic imperatives—"Avenge," "Forget not," "sow"—which keynote the poet's movement from an initial impulse for revenge to more meditated remembrance and then to fully imagined regeneration. Underlying this movement is a vision of revision and reconstruction. Fundamental to it all is radical reversal. God's seed, according to Matthew's prophecy, can only flourish and produce a "hundred-fold" in the "good ground" of him "that heareth the word, and understandeth it" (Matt. 13 : 8 and 23). The "Italian fields" and the tyrannic landowner will have to be purified. The covenant of the sanctified land shall be renewed.

Samson Agonistes

Revenge, the unqualified moral reflex of a passionate mind confronted with wrong, is close to the heart of much of Milton's greatest poetry. In *Samson Agonistes,* revenge, and the desire for it, describe much of the drama's plot and emotion. So much so that the tangled moral judgment of Ezra Pound was moved to cry out against its author's "asinine bigotry, his beastly Hebraism, the coarseness of his mentality." [7] Milton's conception of Samson's revenge is, we must realize, complex. To begin with, Samson Agonistes is no mere private man acting out his pent-up aggressions. The biblical figure of Samson, we know, was for Milton a symbol of the individual acting alone in a more than private capacity. In his answer to Salmasius, Milton described Samson as follows:

> heroic Samson . . . made war single-handed on his masters, and, whether prompted by God or by his own valor, slew at one stroke not one but a host of his country's tyrants, having first made prayer to God for his aid. Samson therefore thought it not impious but pious to kill those masters who were tyrants over his country, even though most of her citizens did not balk at slavery.[8]

The same or very similar sentiments inhabit the center of Milton's dramatic conception of Samson. Milton asks us to

7. *Make It New* (New Haven, 1953), p. 109.
8. *Complete Prose Works,* 4 : i, 402.

understand that Samson is presented as a being whose indi-
viduality is submerged in his public significance:

> I was no private but a person rais'd
> With strength sufficient and command from Heav'n
> To free my Country; . . .
>
> . . . .
> I was to do my part from Heav'n assign'd.
>
> [ll. 1211–17]

In the Christian tradition, we know, revenge or violent re-
dress is not usually given high spiritual grades. But for Milton, Samson's bloody reawakening was a symbol of national
regeneration through revenge; and it was a symbol which was,
for him, especially relevant to his own glorious, half-fallen England. As a younger man the association of his nation with
Samson had inspired him to the level of prophecy:

> Methinks I see in my mind a noble and puissant Nation
> rousing herself like a strong man after sleep, and shaking
> her invincible locks: Methinks I see her as an Eagle
> muing her mighty youth, and . . . unscaling her long
> abused sight at the fountain . . . of heav'nly radiance.[9]

We must, of course, be careful not to foist extraneous consid-
erations onto Milton's dramatic text. What Milton wrote in
Areopagitica in 1644 is not necessarily relevant to what he
wrote two or fifteen or twenty-five years later.[10] But a comparison of the *Areopagitica* image with *Samson Agonistes* di-
rects us to what is, perhaps, the crucial aspect of Milton's
dramatic hero. In the treatise he is not used to image individual salvation but the symbolic self-redemption of an entire
people: England "not degenerated nor drooping to a fatall
decay, but casting off the old and wrincl'd skin of corruption
to outlive . . . pangs and wax young again." [11] The Samson

9. Ibid., 2 : 557–58.
10. I have tried to avoid the controversy that surrounds the dating of
the play. For the sake of convenience I have discussed *Samson Agonistes*
before *Paradise Lost*, though I believe it likely that the drama was
Milton's last work.
11. *Complete Prose Works*, 2 : 557.

of *Areopagitica* is preeminently a figure of public-mythic renewal. Samson Agonistes, who also begins "dark, dark, dark,
amid the blaze" of the full noon beam, is likewise primarily a
figure of public renewal, of regenerated virtuous essence. The
mythic adjuncts of Milton's *Areopagitica* image receive extended and climactic emphasis in the drama:

> he though blind of sight,
> Despis'd and thought extinguish't quite,
> With inward eyes illuminated
> His fiery virtue rous'd
> From under ashes into sudden flame,
>
> . . . .
> . . . as an Eagle
> His cloudless thunder bolted on thir heads.
> So virtue giv'n for lost,
> Deprest, and overthrown, as seem'd,
> Like that self-begott'n bird
> In the *Arabian* woods embost,
> That no second knows nor third,
> And lay erewhile a Holocaust,
> From out her ashy womb now teem'd,
> Revives, reflourishes, then vigorous most
> When most unactive deem'd,
> And though her body die, her fame survives,
> A secular bird ages of lives.
>
> [ll. 1687–1707]

The use of the elaborate phoenix myth as a simile for Samson's rejuvenation suggests a mythic scope far greater than re-
vived personal strength.[12]

What is it, precisely, that is renewed in or by Samson?
Clearly the question is of prime importance for the entire
drama, yet no well-defined answer is provided by the close.
Indeed, Manoa seems intent on frustrating any pat moralizing
on the result of his son's actions: Samson is Samson, he tells us

12. For background to the phoenix image, see Thomas Greene, *The
Descent from Heaven: A Study in Epic Continuity* (New Haven, 1963),
pp. 397–401.

laconically; his heroic deed was typical of his heroism: "*Samson* hath quit himself / Like *Samson*, and heroicly hath finish'd / A life Heroic, on his Enemies / Fully reveng'd" (ll. 1709–12). In perhaps the strangest moment of the entire play, Manoa suggests that the burden of Samson's achievement is in the promise of liberation—the opportunity for augmented rebellion—created by his revenge, which "To Israel / Honor hath left, and freedom, let but them / Find courage to lay hold on this occasion" (ll. 1714–16).

A. S. P. Woodhouse remarked that the drama as a whole narrows its theme to "a specific historical situation and one which at point after point suggests to us, and cannot have failed to suggest to him, Milton's own." [13] Coming as they do, so close to the end of the drama, with no context of organized or organizable resistance to the Philistines, the lines just quoted, with their call to action, seem to leap off the page directly at the bosom of the English reader. Understandably— though, I think, mistakenly—one critic was moved to assert that *Samson Agonistes* actually offers "a dramatization of the apparent death and predicted resurrection of the Good Old Cause." [14] Without doubt a powerful sense of contemporary reality haunts Manoa's words. What can Milton have meant? What is it that rises reborn from the scene of Samson's self-destruction?

In seeking an answer to this question in its various parts, we should remind ourselves that the world of *Samson Agonistes,* a pointedly religious drama, is distinguished by a deliberate exclusion of not only New Testament myth but also the vast Renaissance treasure house of classical mythography. In spite of the Greek form of the work, the reader is rudely reminded that the pagan myths are, after all, fictions: the "Gentiles feign," that Atlas bears up heaven (l. 150); Tantalus is an exemplar of "garrulity," "a sin / That Gentiles in thir Parables condemn / To thir abyss and horrid pains confin'd"

13. *"Samson Agonistes* and Milton's Experience," *Transactions of the Royal Society of Canada* 43 (1949) : 161.

14. E. M. Clark, "Milton's Earlier *Samson*," *University of Texas Studies in English* 7 (1927) : 149.

(ll. 491–501). The effect of this exclusion is not to exorcise all myth, but to narrow the field to two competing myth systems or complexes. Samson's greatest sin, his father compels him to recall, is that while he was chosen by God to further the Hebraic divinity he unwittingly became the sponsor of the Philistian:

> So *Dagon* shall be magnified, and God,
> Besides whom is no God, compar'd with Idols,
> Disglorified, blasphem'd, and had in scorn
> By th' Idolatrous rout amidst thir wine;
> Which to have come to pass by means of thee,
> *Samson,* of all thy sufferings think the heaviest,
> Of all reproach the most with shame that ever
> Could have befall'n thee.
>
> [ll. 440–47]

Samson acknowledges that consciousness of these facts is "my chief affliction, shame and sorrow, / The anguish of my Soul" (ll. 457–58). But he adds, somewhat mysteriously,

> This only hope relieves me, that the strife
> With mee hath end; all the contest is now
> 'Twixt God and *Dagon; Dagon* hath presum'd,
> Mee overthrown, to enter lists with God,
> His Deity comparing and preferring
> Before the God of *Abraham.*
>
> [ll. 460–65]

In ranging Hebraic forces against Philistian, Milton emphasizes the biblical association of sexual transgression with the beginning of Samson's service to Dagon:

> swoll'n with pride into the snare I fell
> Of fair fallacious looks, venereal trains,
> Soft'n'd with pleasure and voluptuous life;
> At length to lay my head and hallow'd pledge
> Of all my strength in the lascivious lap
> Of a deceitful Concubine.
>
> [ll. 532–37]

This causal connection between sexuality and idolatry persists not only in Samson's guilt-ridden mind, as when he speaks
of displaying his strength in honor of Dagon as "prostituting
holy things to Idols" (ll. 1358 ff.), but also comprises major
parts of the contesting myths. Samson, as he himself reminds
us, is a Nazarite especially appointed by God, a being set apart
as an active symbol of God's covenant with *"Abraham's* race,"
his "breeding order'd and prescrib'd / As of a person separate
to God, / Design'd for great exploits" (ll. 29–32). Throughout
the play the reader is reminded that it is the covenant of Abraham, symbolized by the sanctifying circumcision of the male
sexual member, which distinguishes the "unforeskinn'd" Hebrews (l. 1100) from the "Idolatrous uncircumcis'd" Philistines, who are elsewhere simply called "foreskins" (l. 144).[15]
Samson's other marks of covenant are also emphasized repeatedly: part of his charge, for example, was a "sacred trust of
silence" (l. 428); he surrendered his "fort of silence" (l. 236)
through "Shameful garrulity" (l. 491). What emerges is a covenantal myth compounded of fidelity, sexual continence, faith,
and prophetic promise of which the visible sign is Samson's
strength.

E. M. W. Tillyard noted that *Samson Agonistes* is constructed on a principle of rigorously defined Aristotelian peripeteia. A peripeteia occurs, he explained, "not when there is
a mere change of fortune, but when an intention or action
brings about the opposite of what was meant. . . . The essence of the plot in *Samson* is that nearly all the actions
should lead whither they had not seemed to lead." [16] Ironic
reversal in the action of the drama, we should add, is extended
to and complemented by a gradual yet complete inversion of
key terms in Samson's tragic situation, such as blindness and
slavery. If we ask for Samson "now"—that is, at the opening
of the drama—we find him "Eyeless in Gaza at the Mill with
slaves" (ll. 40–41).

But as the dialogue unfolds, and especially as Samson violently denounces Dalila and the slavish sexuality that bound

15. They are twice more described as "uncircumcis'd," at ll. 260 and
640.

16. *Milton* (London, 1930), p. 343.

him to the service of idolaters, his perspective turns inward so that the only liberty which becomes meaningful to him is freedom of the mind and spirit. "This Gaol," he tells Dalila, perhaps with a conviction of only comparative value, "I count the house of Liberty / To thine whose doors my feet shall never enter" (ll. 949–50). When the Philistian officer asks him to reconsider his refusal to appear at the festivities—"Regard thyself," he says, "this will offend them highly" (l. 1333)—Samson answers, now with more absolute self-confidence,

> Myself? my conscience and internal peace.
> Can they think me so broken, so debas'd
> With corporal servitude, that my mind ever
> Will condescend to such absurd commands?
>
> [ll. 1334–37]

As he moves closer and closer to his terminal act of total emancipation, the expressing of God's "uncontrollable intent" (l. 1754), Samson perceives that even his apparent physical servitude will somehow turn out to be less than service to the Philistines. His reversal in conception slowly materializes in action. When his father notes, "with this strength thou serv'st the Philistines" (l. 1363), Samson answers presagefully, "Not in thir Idol-Worship." As he elaborates to himself and to his listeners his understanding of his apparent servitude, he suddenly understands that God

> may dispense with me or thee
> Present in Temples at Idolatrous Rites
> For some important cause, thou needst not doubt.
> . . . .
> I with this Messenger will go along,
> Nothing to do, be sure, that may dishonor
> Our Law, or stain my vow of *Nazarite*.
>
> [ll. 1365–86]

The peripety of thraldom is, of course, closely related to the peripety of blindness, so much so, in fact, that Samson's regenerated definitions of both concepts begin at the same point —with his revulsion at his sexual surrender to Dalila:

O blot
To Honor and Religion! servile mind
Rewarded well with servile punishment!
The base degree to which I now am fall'n,
These rags, this grinding, is not yet so base
As was my former servitude, ignoble,
Unmanly, ignominious, infamous,
True slavery, and that blindness worse than this,
That saw not how degenerately I serv'd.

[ll. 411–19]

Here again the abstract peripety issues in action: the Philistines

thir own ruin on themselves . . . invite,
Insensate left, or to sense reprobate,
And with blindness internal struck.

[ll. 1684–86]

Manoa's prophecy that "God will restore him eyesight to his strength" (l. 1503) is perhaps fulfilled in Samson's last moments between the pillars, when with "eyes fast fixt he stood" (l. 1637).

We see, then, that Tillyard's point about peripeteia applies extensively throughout the play, not only in the reversal of "intention or action" but also in the ironic inversion of concepts that are central to the meaning of the drama. Reversal is the order of the twenty-four-hour day to which *Samson Agonistes* is confined. Yet Tillyard, I think, has missed an important—perhaps even a crucial—aspect of the play in understanding its peripeteia as bringing about merely "the opposite of what was meant." Within the context of *Samson Agonistes,* where the essential tragedy, as Samson says, is that the true faith of Abraham has been momentarily vanquished and displaced by its opposing mythos, the degenerate idolatry of Dagon, reversal to the opposite of Philistian intention means *return to covenant,* that is, regeneration to something which is present, though latent, all along.

In fact, the dramatic vitality of *Samson Agonistes* depends on a prophetic peripety to something that is present from the beginning of the play, though readers have for some reason been oblivious to its dramatic significance. I refer to the mysteriously elusive outward manifestation of Samson's strength, his old-new

> redundant lock
> Robustious to no purpose clust'ring down,
> Vain monument of strength.
>
> [ll. 568–70]

In these lines Samson suggests that his full strength is a thing of the past, that his locks are deficient in the virtue of which they were shorn. Though he still has strength "surpassing human rate" (l. 1313) wherewith to serve his Philistian taskmasters in the "work of many hands" (l. 1260), Samson is a fallen Atlas condemned to prop up the powers that now rule his world (cf. l. 150).

Milton was left a large measure of latitude by the terse biblical text, which tells us no more than that "the hair of his head began to grow again after he was shaven" (Judges 16 : 22). It was up to Milton to specify when and how much of Samson's pilicentric strength returns at exactly which moment of the tragedy. Milton's savoring of this opportunity indicates that in composing *Samson Agonistes* he did not simply settle for closet drama; rather, he exploited and relied upon a technical agility of the reader's imagination that no live stage could possibly have matched. Though we hear again and again that Samson still has "Heav'n-gifted strength" (l. 36), that he has "strength / Miraculous yet remaining in those locks" (ll. 586–87), we are not allowed to know precisely how much of his strength he has regained; until the very last moments there is no indication of its extent. Clearly, Samson's Philistian captors have only a very imperfect idea of his physical state when they order him into their festive midst to "heave" and "break"; and when they allow him to rest between the mainstays of their cavernous hall we cannot assume that they have made a daring calculation of his unwillingness to include himself in a general destruction. They are blinded by hubris, and one of the things they do not see, and have not been allowed to see earlier, is the full length and luster of Samson's locks.

Manoa's ignorance of the divine process to which his son's life has been committed is nowhere more meaningfully ironic than in his estimate, early and late, of Samson's strength. After first seeing Samson, he declares him

> now unequal match
> To save himself against a coward arm'd
> At one spear's length.
>
> [ll. 346–48]

Even the details of Manoa's challenging fight regulations are complied with when the heavyweight coward, Harapha, appears in the ring and Samson vanquishes him—precisely at spear's-length—with his breath:

> I only with an Oak'n staff will meet thee,
> And raise such outcries on thy clatter'd Iron,
> Which long shall not withhold me from thy head
> . . . .
> Then thou shalt see, or rather to thy sorrow
> Soon feel, whose God is strongest, thine or mine.
>
> [ll. 1123–55]

Yet we should not be too quick to relish Manoa's opacity. No one in the play, including Samson himself, is quite sure how much of his strength has returned until the very end. A purposeful mystery shrouds Samson's head. When he tells the chorus, at the beginning of the play, that the common rout "Immeasurable strength . . . might behold / In me" (ll. 206–07), we cannot know the tense of "might behold." The chorus's much later statement to Samson that

> never was from Heaven imparted
> Measure of strength so great to mortal seed,
> As in thy wond'rous actions hath been seen
>
> [ll. 1438–40]

similarly implies deliberately vague temporal limits.

Judged within this context, Dr. Johnson's assertion that

"nothing passes between the first act and the last, that either
hastens or delays the Death of Samson" [17] must be considered
mistaken. Something is happening. We strain with the eyes of
our imaginations when Samson says to Harapha,

> My trust is in the living God who gave me
> At my Nativity this strength, diffus'd
> No less through all my sinews, joints and bones,
> Than thine, while I preserv'd these locks unshorn
> The pledge of my unviolated vow.
>
> [ll. 1140–45]

Equation of his strength with Harapha's takes away the promise of "this strength." The next two phrases vibrate between
polar opposites: the locks have been shorn, yet they are present enough to be described as "these"; the vow has been violated, yet the conviction and challenge of the statement suggest that it has been renewed. Samson is toying with Harapha,
with the reader, and perhaps, agonizingly, with himself. Much
of the dramatic tension of the play is generated by his painfully uncertain assessment of his condition. When Manoa suggests that God must have some providential purpose for his
"strength / . . . yet remaining" (ll. 586–87), Samson reports
that his strength is waning: "nature within me seems / In all
her functions weary of herself" (ll. 595–96). His strength resides on the misty border between material force and spiritual energy. Only God's "Secret refreshings [can] repair his
strength, / And fainting spirits uphold" (ll. 665–66). Samson's
"rousing motions" (l. 1382) are one part muscle, one part
psyche, and one part prophecy. As onlookers, we can only be
sure that his strength and locks are growing before our very
eyes and that this, whatever it reflects, is part of the chief action of the play. Samson only gradually becomes aware of the
mystery that is enveloping him:

> Shall I abuse this Consecrated gift
> Of strength, again returning with my hair

17. *The Rambler*, no. 139, in *The Yale Edition of the Works of Samuel
Johnson*, ed. E. L. McAdam, Jr. et al. (New Haven, 1969), 4 : 376.

After my great transgression, so requite
Favor renew'd . . . ?

[ll. 1354–56]

As spectators of the carefully structured peripeteia, we are
meant to sense from the start—from the first ambiguous refer-
ences to Samson's strength and from our first efforts to visualize his shorn head—that Samson's locks will fall into a different configuration from the one expected, that they will
themselves return, and that the dénouement of the tragedy
will somehow consist of "returning."

But what of the *anagnorisis* or "recognition" which issues
from the peripeteia? The question, in any form we choose to
frame it, is extremely important. Woodhouse asked, "Is it true
that our sense of [the catastrophe's] place in a providential
scheme, and of Samson as a divine instrument, dwarfs the human drama of Samson the man?" In spite of Woodhouse's
(and many others') desire to view *Samson Agonistes* as a Christian tragedy concerned with individual grace and redemption,
we must answer yes to his question: Samson is absorbed into,
and therefore dwarfed by, a larger goal of group renewal. We
must not forget that, even after all typological interpretations
of the play have been piled high, there is still lacking even a
shred of explicit Christian doctrine in the text itself.[18]

What was it, then, that Sir Richard Jebb sensed seventy
years ago when he vexed so many later scholars to nightmare
by asserting that the play is an exemplar of Hebraism? [19] If

18. *"Samson Agonistes* and Milton's Experience," pp. 167 ff. For the
typological view of the play, see F. Michael Krouse, *Milton's Samson and
the Christian Tradition* (Princeton, 1949). Marjorie Hope Nicolson, in
John Milton: A Reader's Guide to His Poetry (New York, 1963), p. 352,
has remarked, "I myself do not feel the drama Christian. Its great power
in my mind lies in the very fact that it is the least Christian of all Milton's major works, indeed that Christianity plays almost no part in it.
Milton is at his greatest when he treats the Old Testament rather than
the New (with a few exceptions when he paraphrases the Book of Reve-
lation). . . . *Samson Agonistes* combines the two great cultures [classical
and Hebraic] to which Milton was most responsive."

19. *"Samson Agonistes* and the Hellenic Drama," *Proceedings of the
British Academy* 3 (1903) : 341.

the drift of what I have been arguing is correct, such descriptions point to the fact that in large part the anagnorisis of the tragedy is not Samson's but ours: it belongs to us inasmuch as we are the inheritors of Milton's contemporary audience. We are undoubtedly meant to imagine that in his last moments of prayer and last seconds of existence Samson was able to understand a good deal of God's intent. But the "morning Trumpets" of the Philistines have "proclaim'd" primarily to us (cf. l. 1598). Samson fulfills himself by gradually recovering the signs of his covenant with God. In the moment after death, surrounded by the rubble of Philistian doom, he even regains his "fort of silence." But the anagnorisis of his tragic peripeteia is not primarily personal. Individual salvation or justification is a hazy tangent to the drama's inner circle of attention. More even than an individuated symbol of regenerating England, Samson represents regained public consciousness of covenantal power and destiny. Samson's strength is not so much his own as that of God's covenant with Israel: it lurks mysteriously in the wings, ready to become operative when the conditions that keep the covenant in force are fulfilled.

In Samson, Milton saw an opportunity for penetrating to a pristine source of divine, depersonalized vision of present and future. The protagonist's "magnitude of mind" embraces vast public dimensions; it is "Heroic" because it subserves the suprapersonal (cf. l. 1279). *Samson Agonistes* images the regeneration of a mythic covenant. The regeneration reaches fullness in the "calm of mind" (l. 1758) of the auditors, Israel-England, who have traced the recurring peripety of Samson's God: "Oft he seems to hide his face, / But unexpectedly returns" (ll. 1749–50). It is now up to them to lay hold on this occasion and to stand once again in the presence of the "living Dread who dwells / In Silo" (ll. 1673–74).

Paradise Lost

There may be some truth in Thomas Ellwood's story that when, after being allowed to read the completed manuscript of *Paradise Lost,* he suggested to Milton that he now write "Paradise Found," the relaxing poet was so affected by the

remark that he "sat some time in a muse." [20] It is possible that
Milton had begun to hope that readers would eagerly seek out
the "Paradise, far happier . . . / Than this of Eden" (12. 464–
65) which was a great part of the bitterly won burden of his
magnum opus. He had every reason to be taken aback by Ellwood's bright idea. Much of the power of *Paradise Lost* arises
from the overarching irony that the narrative of desolation is
at the same time a scaffolding of reconstruction. Though the
scaffolding itself is comprised of aspects of the poem that have
already benefited from voluminous commentary, it will be useful to view them in a light not usually shone on Milton.

The reconstructive procedures of *Paradise Lost* are of many
kinds. They consist partly in explicit rehabilitations of words
and phrases that have earlier gone to the devil's party. Mam-
mon's boast, for example, that the greatness of the Satanic host

> will appear
> Then most conspicuous, when great things of small,
> Useful of hurtful, prosperous of adverse
> We can create, and in what place soe'er
> Thrive under evil,
>
> [2. 257–61]

reappears, transfigured and purified, in the rueful words of
Adam, another fallen creature, but one who is repentant:

> Henceforth I learn . . .
> . . . .
> . . . To observe
> His providence, and on him sole depend,
> Merciful over all his works, with good
> Still overcoming evil, and by small
> Accomplishing great things.
>
> [12. 561–67]

Redisposition of a more extensive kind is found in the careful anatomizing and resynthesis of entire passages. The seduc-
ing dream, for example, that Satan breathes in at Eve's ear
was clearly created for such processing:

20. Ellwood's account is quoted at length—and rejected on grounds I
have adopted here—by Tillyard, *Milton*, pp. 297–98.

Why sleep'st thou *Eve?* now is the pleasant time,
The cool, the silent, save where silence yields
To the night-warbling Bird, that now awake
Tunes sweetest his love-labor'd song; now reigns
Full Orb'd the Moon, and with more pleasing light
Shadowy sets off the face of things; in vain,
If none regard; Heav'n wakes with all his eyes,
Whom to behold but thee, Nature's desire

. . . .

And O fair Plant . . . with fruit surcharg'd,
Deigns none to ease thy load and taste thy sweet,
Nor God, nor Man; is knowledge so despis'd?

. . . .

              . . . O Fruit Divine,
Sweet of thyself, but much more sweet thus cropt,
Forbidd'n here, it seems, as only fit
For Gods, yet able to make Gods of Men.

                              [5. 38–70]

Before engaging in the act of revision itself, Adam explains precisely what the available tools are. A good deal of the intellectual aspiration of *Paradise Lost*—of its attempt to redeem reason from fancy and the senses—is mirrored in Adam's schema of the regenerate human mind, which he explains to Eve not merely to comfort her, but to teach her how to deal with fancy's inundations:

            know that in the Soul
      Are many lesser Faculties that serve
      Reason as chief; among these Fancy next
      Her office holds; of all external things,
      Which the five watchful Senses represent,
      She forms Imaginations, Aery shapes,
      Which Reason joining or disjoining, frames
      All what we affirm or what deny.

                              [5. 100–07]

Reinforced with this knowledge, Eve can bow with Adam in matin wakening to true consciousness (5. 153–208). Their reason-controlled imaginations offer a paradigm of the disjoining and joining of that which "misjoining" fancy and some "addition strange" have injected as "Evil into the mind of . . . Man" (cf. 5. 110 ff.). Reason begins by shifting the center of orientation from man and nature to God the creator; reason "frames" with God's "Frame":

> These are thy glorious works, Parent of good,
> Almighty, thine this universal Frame,
> Thus wondrous fair; thyself how wondrous then!
>
> [5. 153–55]

Those elements which Satan has combined into temptation are not in themselves evil. Adam's and Eve's purpose in prayer is, as they say, to "Vary to our great Maker still new praise" (5. 184), on the Platonic assumption that all things in nature, like the elements of matter themselves, are (as Merritt Hughes has phrased it) "reversibly transformable": [21]

> Elements the eldest birth
> Of Nature's Womb . . . in quaternion run
> Perpetual Circle, multiform, and mix
> And nourish all things.
>
> [5. 180–83]

Satan's sensuous description of the "pleasant time . . . cool . . . silent" is sublimed into "Mists and Exhalations" which "In honor to the World's great Author rise" (5. 185–88), while our first parents shatter the silence of obliviousness—both man's and nature's—to God:

> Witness if I be silent, Morn or Even,
> To Hill, or Valley, Fountain, or fresh shade
> Made vocal by my Song, and taught his praise.
>
> [5. 202–04]

Satan's reigning moon is shown to be less than the sun, which is itself asked to acknowledge God "thy Greater, sound his praise" (5. 172). None of the objects that Satan glorified are condemned; they are only rearranged, subordinated, and made

21. *John Milton: Complete Poems*, p. 306 n.

to proclaim God's creative authority. Even night and darkness
are not located in an enemy camp. Man must simply remind
himself that, though night and lapse of color and consciousness unavoidably overcome man, God persists in "Day without
Night" (5. 162). His high praise, we hear, is that He "out of
Darkness call'd up Light" (5. 179). Compared to God, none
of his earthly creations can be called divine. Satan's elevation
of the "fair Plant" and its "Fruit Divine" is nicely reduced
and comprehended in a subordinate clause within a subordinate thought: "and wave your tops, ye Pines, / With every
Plant, in sign of Worship wave" (5. 193–94). Satan's "night-
warbling Bird" with its "love-labor'd song," a song of self and
of creaturely adoration, is returned to a daylight orison of
divine praise, divine love:

> ye Birds,
> That singing up to Heaven Gate ascend,
> Bear on your wings and in your notes his praise.
>
> [5. 197–99]

In other words, Satan's entire score of usurpation has been re-
written, in every note, into praise of God.

The largest, most conspicuous process of reconstruction in
Paradise Lost is carried out in what we might regard as an
integrated renovation of the materials, causation, and teleol-
ogy of mythic thought. It is a process that has great significance for the meaning of *Paradise Lost* and reflects, by the by,
on the consistency of Milton's later poetical career. Students
and critics have often been shocked by Milton's forthright re-
pudiation of the classical tradition in *Paradise Regained*.
What strange and sudden impulse, it has been asked, could
have moved Milton to assign the entire classical heritage to
Satan—and in such devilishly moving language (cf. *Paradise
Regained*, 4. 236 ff.)? But the evidence of *Samson Agonistes*
suggests that though Milton would not, perhaps could not,
discard the classical reliquaries he had loved so long, he had
determined to cleanse and refill them. He labored to turn the
best of the classical legacy into something biblical. This effort
of reform is reflected in Milton's turning from the composite

Christian-humanist mythography of the *Nativity Ode* and
Lycidas to the severely limited mythographic framework of
Samson. The same deliberate reformation of classical form
and a similarly austere (though different) truncation of classical
mythology take place in *Paradise Lost*—and to the same end.

The Satan of *Paradise Lost* has already been granted title
to a good deal of the classical estate. When he speaks (even at
his most degraded), he is said to remind us of an "Orator renown'd / In Athens or free Rome" (9. 670–71). When he
moves, he is assigned the fullest epic dimensions of a Jason or
Ulysses:

> [He] Springs upward like a Pyramid of fire
> Into the wild expanse, and through the shock
> Of fighting Elements, on all sides round
> Environ'd wins his way; harder beset
> And more endanger'd, than when *Argo* pass'd
> Through *Bosporus* betwixt the justling Rocks:
> Or when *Ulysses* on the Larboard shunn'd
> *Charybdis*, and by th' other whirlpool steer'd.
>
> [2. 1013–20]

As D. C. Allen has recently remarked, "The hellions are Hel-
lenes." [22] Satan's armies embrace and exceed the total martial
grandeur of epic and romance, including even Arthurian legend (here again *Paradise Lost* anticipates *Paradise Regained*
—cf. 2. 360 ff.—this time in its rejection of paganized Christian themes):

> never since created man,
> Met such imbodied force . . .
>
> . . . .
> . . . though all the Giant brood
> Of *Phlegra* with th' Heroic Race were join'd
> That fought at *Thebes* and *Ilium*, on each side
> Mixt with auxiliar Gods; and what resounds

22. Don Cameron Allen, *Mysteriously Meant: The Rediscovery of
Pagan Symbolism and Allegorical Interpretation in the Renaissance* (Baltimore, 1970), p. 294.

In Fable or *Romance* of *Uther's* Son
Begirt with *British* and *Armoric* Knights;
And all who since, Baptiz'd or Infidel
Jousted in *Aspramont* or *Montalban*,
Damasco, or *Marocco,* or *Trebisond.*

[1. 573–84]

There is no eluding the condemnation of traditional heroism implicit in the comparison of Satan with epic heroism.[23]
This heroic tradition, Michael notes, is one in which

> Might only shall be admir'd,
> And Valor and Heroic Virtue call'd;
> To overcome in Battle, and subdue
> Nations, and bring home spoils with infinite
> Man-slaughter, shall be held the highest pitch
> Of human Glory, and for Glory done
> Of triumph, to be styl'd great Conquerors,
> Patrons of Mankind, Gods, and Sons of Gods,
> Destroyers rightlier call'd and Plagues of men.
> Thus Fame shall be achiev'd, renown on Earth.

[11. 689–98]

The poet's own direct comment removes any doubts we might
have about the applicability of this renunciation to the whole
of the classical epic heritage: "hitherto," he says, "Wars" have
been "the only Argument / Heroic deem'd," though they are
decidedly "Not that which justly gives Heroic name / To Person or to Poem" (9. 28–41). Something else must be tried. Like
Juvenal, Milton has come to be repelled by the epic past. He
has committed himself to producing heroic poetry, but he,
too, renounces what has till now passed for heroic action and
matter. It may be that we even hear an echo of Juvenal's first
satire and its climactic refusal to set Aeneas and King Turnus
"a-fighting" or to retell the old harmless story of Achilles's
end—"securus licet Aeneam Rutulumque ferocem / commit-

23. For comment on this condemnation, see C. M. Bowra, *From Virgil
to Milton* (London, 1948), pp. 233–36 and John M. Steadman, *Milton and
the Renaissance Hero* (Oxford, 1967), pp. 177–201.

tas, nulli gravis est percussus Achilles" (1. 162–63)—in Milton's insistence that his argument is

> Not less but more Heroic than the wrath
> Of stern *Achilles* on his Foe pursu'd
> Thrice Fugitive about *Troy* Wall; or rage
> Of *Turnus* for *Lavinia* disespous'd.
>
> [9. 14–17]

Milton's refusal to recirculate this false epic currency is, like Juvenal's, part of an aesthetic of demythology—of melting down, purifying, and reissuing the ancient epic sterling. We must not mistake the renunciation for a wholesale rejection. The larger procedure of this kind of heroic poetry depends on setting an extraordinarily high value upon the impulses and imaginings that produced lapsed epic in the first place.

Paradise Lost is an epic in more than a formal sense. Much of its substance derives from a process of remonetization. To take a prime example, it is probably true that it is difficult or impossible to *visualize* Milton's Paradise. The image is an oblique one, accorded substantiality of a very special kind. Its fields and hills are successor images, supplanting patterns reclaimed from the classically cultivated furrows and convolutions of Western man's myth-apprehending imagination. Without Ovid's Hesperides, Milton's "far more pleasant Garden," with its center-point of "vegetable Gold" (4. 215–20), could hardly be made to exist for us. Eden is conjured to life in the conventional description of

> Groves whose rich Trees wept odorous Gums and Balm,
> Others whose fruit burnisht with Golden Rind
> Hung amiable, *Hesperian* Fables true,
> If true, here only;
>
> [4. 248–51]

or in Satan's distant, anticipatory glimpse of

> other Worlds,
> Or other Worlds they seem'd, or happy Isles,
> Like those *Hesperian* Gardens fam'd of old,

> Fortunate Fields, and Groves and flow'ry Vales,
> Thrice happy Isles.[24]
>
> [3. 566–70]

The truth of pagan fable, widely famed but of hazy origins,
is denied only to be retrieved for the use of biblical, Christian
epic. A similar procedure is applied to other classical materials, which are included, we realize, not to provide graceful
ornamentation but to yield up the true stuff of Paradise they
contain:

> Not that fair field,
> Of *Enna,* where *Proserpin* gath'ring flow'rs
> Herself a fairer Flow'r by gloomy *Dis*
> Was gather'd, which cost *Ceres* all that pain
> To seek her through the world; nor that sweet Grove
> Of *Daphne* by *Orontes,* and th' inspir'd
> *Castalian* Spring might with this Paradise
> Of *Eden* strive.
>
> [4. 268–75]

From a Christian perspective, this imaginative reconversion
is only right and just. "Like his contemporaries," D. C. Allen
remarks, the later Milton saw a "sort of faded biblical story
or demonically perverted history in classical myth." [25] In
Paradise Lost Milton revives and revises pagan myths in order
to discover the biblical myth that is the source of all valuable
mythmaking. The description of the being whom "Men call'd
. . . *Mulciber*" is an outstanding example of this activity:

> how he fell
> From Heav'n, they fabl'd, thrown by angry *Jove*
> Sheer o'er the Crystal Battlements: . . .
>
> . . . .

24. D. C. Allen, *Mysteriously Meant,* pp. 292–93, offers interesting comments on Milton's use of the Hesperian gardens.

25. Ibid., p. 290. Earlier useful discussions of these attitudes are available in Davis P. Harding, *Milton and the Renaissance Ovid* (Urbana,
Ill., 1946), pp. 67 ff., Richard Chase, *Quest for Myth* (Baton Rouge, La.,
1949), pp. 3 ff., and Isabel Gamble MacCaffrey, Paradise Lost *as "Myth"*
(Cambridge, Mass., 1959), pp. 12 ff.

> . . . thus they relate,
> Erring; for he with this rebellious rout
> Fell long before . . .
> . . . .
> . . . headlong sent
> With his industrious crew to build in hell.
>
> [1. 740–51]

But we must emphasize that this is only one, easily recognized
instance of a general mythographic principle (or combination
of principles) whose subtle workings allow us to detect the
"infection" of human imagination that substitutes "wand'ring
Gods"—an Apis or a golden calf—for Jehovah (1. 476 ff.), or
which deifies

> *Ionian* Gods, of *Javan's* Issue held
> Gods, yet confest later than Heav'n and Earth
> Thir boasted Parents.
>
> [1. 508–10]

Milton's description of these gods emphasizes the impulse of
displacement which not only generated the fallacious beginnings of pagan mythology but which is also operative within
it:

> *Titan* Heav'n's first born
> With his enormous brood, and birthright seiz'd
> By younger *Saturn,* he from mightier *Jove*
> His own and *Rhea's* Son like measure found;
> So *Jove* usurping reign'd: . . .
> . . . .
> . . . *Saturn* old
> Fled over *Adria* to th' *Hesperian* Fields.
>
> [1. 510–20]

Here, too, the Hesperian gardens are the symbolic point of
continuity between the half-true world of derivative mythologies and the Edenic reality which is their displaced source.
If we return to the visual image of Paradise—this time survey-

ing its hills—we can perhaps now appreciate more fully the
significance Milton attaches to his displacing muse. With her
help he can fly from "Sion Hill / . . . Above th' Aonian
Mount" and delight in "Siloa's Brook" (1. 10 ff.). The location
of his muse and the image of Eden emerge from a joint redemption of the degenerated images of Parnassus and the
Castalian spring:

> not the more
> Cease I to wander where the Muses haunt
> Clear Spring, or shady Grove, or Sunny Hill,
> Smit with the love of sacred Song; but chief
> Thee *Sion* and the flow'ry Brooks beneath
> That wash thy hallow'd feet, and warbling flow,
> Nightly I visit.
>
> [3. 26–32]

The "Hill / Of Paradise the highest" (11. 377–78), from
which Michael shows Adam the future of his progeny is, in an
essential sense, the very same spot—though sanctified and ele-
vated—as the rising ground from which Aeneas saw into the
future. In fact, the image of geographic holiness offered by
Paradise Lost is a conglomerate of the haunts of Milton's
muse, of the territories it has reconquered from pagan inroads,
and of a "later" collateral spiritual topography also involved
in patterns of displacement. A good example of this last phenomenon is the "opprobrious Hill" on which Solomon was
"led by fraud to build" Moloch's temple "right against the
Temple of God" (1. 401–03). Ripples of the same image pattern are noticeable in the description of the cult of Astarte and
Thammuz. Worship of their images, we are told, usurped the
worship of the true Deity on his hill of holiness.[26] Within the
account of the pagan cults themselves, a structure of displacing
myth is repeatedly emphasized. To Astarte

---

26. Maud Bodkin, *Archetypal Patterns in Poetry: Psychological Studies
of Imagination* (London, 1934), pp. 99 ff. and MacCaffrey, Paradise Lost
as "Myth," pp. 44 ff., discuss Milton's mythic mountains from other, related points of view.

Sidonian Virgins paid thir Vows and Songs,
In *Sion* also not unsung, where stood
Her Temple on th' offensive Mountain, built
By that uxorious King, whose heart though large,
Beguil'd by fair Idolatresses, fell
To Idols foul. *Thammuz* came next behind,
Whose annual wound in *Lebanon* allur'd
The *Syrian* Damsels to lament his fate
In amorous ditties all a Summer's day,
While smooth *Adonis* from his native Rock
Ran purple to the Sea, suppos'd with blood
Of *Thammuz* yearly wounded: the Love-tale
Infected *Sion's* daughters with like heat,
Whose wanton passions in the sacred Porch
Ezekiel saw, when by the Vision led
His eye survey'd the dark Idolatries
Of alienated *Judah.*

[1. 441–57]

Like Ezekiel on the Temple Mount (8 : 13–14), Milton observes the spreading infection that is the cause of alienation from God. The heat and wanton passions of Sion's daughters remind the reader of the heat and passion, later to be made explicit, of their first mother, through whose transgression earth first "felt the wound" (9. 782). Like Ezekiel, Milton can rise to "Vision" in the process of destroying the infectious "Love-tale" that has its dim origins in divine truth, the high truth which is Milton's biblical love-tale.

With some cause, readers have wondered why, in the invocation to book 7, Milton persists in calling his muse "Urania" if she is, as he asserts, only "an empty dream" (7. 39). But we must understand that for Milton to soar "above th' Olympian Hill" (7. 3) he must, according to the logic of his poetic situation and his poetic program, begin with the classical dream-heritage bequeathed him by man's distorting, "misjoining" fancy (cf. 5. 100 ff.). The poet's faith is that the ancient dream contains a still more ancient reality, that within the airy myth resides one of divine substance, and that—most difficult article of all—a great fiction must harbor a great, salvageable truth even if the fiction and the truth are very opposites. This last tenet, which holds out the larger justification for the epic presentation of Satan and Hell, is the formal literary counterpart of the poem's moral-poetic creed. If there is a central principle of causation in *Paradise Lost,* it is that good ultimately comes of evil, that moral energy inevitably emerges from perverted power, and that higher forms eventually escape the degenerated casings which enclose them. God's purpose is "Good out of evil to create" (7. 188), and "evil turn to good" (12. 471). Behind it all is an assumption that the world began with good and with transcendent form and that communal and private moral life is a struggle of recovery and liberation. Paradise always abides "within."

This is not the place for yet another disquisition on the problem of Satanism—Milton's or the critics'. But if we assume that a large (perhaps the largest) part of the difficulty many readers encounter with *Paradise Lost's* moral structure is Satan's epic, heroic, classical status, it is clear that Milton granted him, or rather degraded him to, that status in order to deny both his value and, reciprocally, the face value of the epic tradition. It has often been argued that Milton's Satan had to be presented as an imposing figure in order that God might have a dramatically convincing opponent. This is true, but perhaps less important than the strategy of displacement that required Satan's imposing appearance for what it could contribute to the ultimate image of greatness in *Paradise Lost* —insofar as fallen man is at all capable of perceiving such an image. The ruins of Satan's demi-heroic deportment, with its straining after individual identity and total liberty, become part of the imaginative building material of everything good and truly heroic in Milton's epic. This is as true of Satan as epic myth, as it is true of the mythic principle of convertibility he espouses: "The mind is its own place, and in itself / Can make a Heav'n of Hell, a Hell of Heav'n" (1. 254–55). Though for Satan "all good" does become psychological "Bane" (cf. 9.

122–23), he himself realizes that the ordained process of God's universe flows in the opposite direction. It is this inevitability which he yearns to thwart:

> If then his Providence
> Out of our evil seek to bring forth good,
> Our labor must be to pervert that end,
> And out of good still to find means of evil.
>
> [1. 162–65]

Yet all Satan's "malice," we know early in the poem, "serv'd but to bring forth / Infinite goodness" (1. 217–18).

Satan's mythic status, for all its impressiveness, is made an instrument for propagating a higher myth. His energies and designs are, in Milton's theodicy, woven into a comprehensive mythic pattern of human and cosmic destiny. The description of his legions on the burning lake is a good example of this patterning. They lie

> Thick as Autumnal Leaves that strow the Brooks
> In *Vallombrosa,* where th' *Etrurian* shades
> High overarch't imbow'r; or scatter'd sedge
> Afloat, when with fierce Winds *Orion* arm'd
> Hath vext the Red-Sea Coast, whose waves o'erthrew
> *Busiris* and his *Memphian* Chivalry,
> While with perfidious hatred they pursu'd
> The Sojourners of *Goshen,* who beheld
> From the safe shore thir floating Carcasses.
>
> [1. 302–10]

Satanic force is unable to interfere with the progress of God's promised conversion of evil into good, symbolized by the Mosaic march out of Egypt. Milton's chosen metaphor grafts Satan's withering host, will they nill they, onto a pattern of inexorable causation: his fallen angels are "Autumnal Leaves" —decaying evil's rich compost—shaken off from God's great-rooted blossomer, which elsewhere continues to thrive.

In fact, one of the most prominent image patterns in the poem, the movement from fallen or plucked fruit to nascent seed, becomes in *Paradise Lost* an insistent symbol of causal

displacement. Even in the epic's exordium "the Fruit / Of that
Forbidden Tree," once pulled down and ruptured, disperses
not only "all our woe" but also "the chosen Seed" of divine
promise (1. 1–8). In eating the forbidden fruit, Adam and Eve
destroyed for themselves a mystery of limit and authority that
funtioned as the nucleus of their spiritual economy. But God's
mercy does not allow the myth to decompose and pass away.
The dead fruit produces a seed and a new fruit which reem-
body the original mythic consciousness in a mystery of suffering
and repentance. This process is readily observable in the restoration of Adam's fallen mind in Christ's presentation of man's
contrition. The reader is made witness to a reflection of the
moment in which the greater Man restores us (cf. 1. 4 ff.).
Adam's first words after the fateful bite were,

> *Eve,* now I see thou art exact of taste,
> And elegant, of Sapience no small part,
> Since to each meaning savor we apply,
> And Palate call judicious; I the praise
> Yield thee, so well this day thou hast purvey'd.
>
> [9. 1017–21]

God's providential displacement of evil with good is reflected
in Christ's rearrangement of Adam's exclamation. The greater
Man, with eyes focused on God rather than on Eve, *sees* for
man again; man's misdirected praise is redirected; the violated
fruit springs anew; gross "meaning savor" becomes "more
pleasing savor"; "elegance" becomes "implanted Grace":

> See Father, what first fruits on Earth are sprung
> From thy implanted Grace in Man, these Sighs
> And Prayers, which in this Golden Censer, mixt
> With Incense, I thy Priest before thee bring,
> Fruits of more pleasing savor from thy seed
> Sown with contrition in his heart, than those
> Which his own hand manuring all the Trees
> Of Paradise could have produc't, ere fall'n
> From innocence.
>
> [11. 22–30]

The new-sown seed, issue of fatal fruit, is the culminating metaphor of *Paradise Lost*. In it is somehow comprehended both the doom of Satan and the promise of Eve's progeny. In book 10 its germinating configuration is sketched only in "mysterious terms, judg'd as then best" (l. 173): "Her Seed shall bruise thy head," Satan hears, "thou bruise his heel" (l. 181). But it is not Milton's intention to drape his essential meaning in Saïslike shrouds. Far from being "an untransmuted lump of futurity," as C. S. Lewis thought, books 11 and 12 are an attempt to translate mythic truths, which have become so obscure as to seem irrelevant, into communicable form. If it is true that Milton's presentation of divinity in *Paradise Lost* is not "sufficiently awful, mysterious, and vague" [27] to put it beyond the reach of rational approach and criticism, it is because a vital part of his purpose in the poem is to reunite the mysterious and the rational in disentangled, refurbished myths. Adam's initial misunderstanding of the seed prophecy must be revised: his belief that he and Eve will ambush Satan and find "revenge indeed" by being allowed to "crush his head" (10. 1031 ff.) represents a primitive conception of the mysteries of iniquity and salvation. The fundamental mysteriousness is never denied, but it is, in various ways, explicated to make Adam aware of the complex, simultaneous referents of the myth:

> by that Seed
> Is meant thy great deliverer, who shall bruise
> The Serpent's head; whereof to thee anon
> Plainlier shall be reveal'd.
>
> [12. 148–51]

Our first parents must be informed

> by types
> And shadows, of that destin'd Seed to bruise
> The Serpent, by what means he shall achieve
> Mankind's deliverance.
>
> [12. 232–35]

In *Paradise Lost*, as in "On the Late Massacre" and *Samson Agonistes*, the obverse and issue of prophesied revenge is

27. *A Preface to* Paradise Lost (London, 1942), pp. 125–26.

divine promise or covenantal renewal. Throughout the later part of the epic the two themes come closer and closer together. They are, in fact, both part of the same myth expressed in the same image. Michael is told to

> reveal
> To *Adam* what shall come in future days,
> As I shall thee enlighten, intermix
> My Cov'nant in the woman's seed renew'd.
>
> [11. 113–16]

The myth of *Paradise Lost* is presented in a process of unraveling and proclamation. It is a discipline that conditions the attentive reader in a manner analogous to the method that leads Adam and Eve to the "better Cov'nant, disciplin'd / From shadowy Types to Truth" (12. 302–03). We need no special knowledge of sevententh-century typological conventions to understand, for example, that the Adam who sees an angel "through the spicy Forest onward come" (5. 298) is offered an adumbration of the covenant promised to Abraham's seed and of the Annunciation. Abraham will see the Lord approaching from afar to inform him and his mate that their seed "shall surely become a great and mighty nation, and all the nations of the earth shall be blessed in him" (Genesis 18 : 1– 18). Three times the reader hears that in Adam's seed, passed on through Abraham, "All Nations shall be blest" (12. 125– 26).[28] When the reader's imagination penetrates the "meaning," "savoury fruits" (5. 304) that Eve prepares for "Phoenix" Raphael (cf. 5. 272), he sees the projected shadow of the promised seed. The image of the Phoenix cycle is itself subtly absorbed into the metaphor of seed renewal, as, for example, in Book 3 when God foretells that "The World shall burn, and from her ashes spring / New Heav'n and Earth, wherein the just shall dwell" (ll. 334–35). The spring of the fabled bird and the growth of the divine stock are merged in an image which is, like the postdeluvian rainbow, meant to

---

28. Cf. 12 : 147–48 and 150. It is interesting to note that the first printed line of Milton's English verse (a translation of Psalm 114, undertaken at age fifteen) concerns "the blest seed of *Terah's* faithful Son."

> call to mind his Cov'nant: Day and Night,
> Seed-time and Harvest, Heat and hoary Frost
> Shall hold thir course, till fire purge all things new,
> Both Heav'n and Earth, wherein the just shall dwell.
>
> [11. 898–901]

As in the myth of Plato's *Politicus,* God's withdrawal to his conning tower attends upon a dramatic reversal in the order of the world, though in *Paradise Lost* the withdrawal is less absolute and is presented more as a symptom than as a cause of degeneration. The danger described is the same, as is the remedy: in those few, God's remnant, for whom forgetfulness of the former divine ordinance is not total, lies man's only hope of recovery from his periodic plunge toward chaos:

> Thus will this latter, as the former World,
> Still tend from bad to worse, till God at last
> Wearied with their iniquities, withdraw
> His presence from among them, and avert
> His holy Eyes; resolving from thenceforth
> To leave them to thir own polluted ways;
> And one peculiar Nation to select
> From all the rest, of whom to be invok'd,
> A Nation from one faithful man to spring.
>
> [12. 105–13]

Periodically the Satanic perversion of man's true heroic impulse takes over. Nimrod, the anticivilizer, is an exemplum of the pagan heroic myth gone mad. He is seen to displace and "arrogate Dominion" by force of arms and tyranny (12. 24 ff.). His usurpation is the physical counterpart of the priestly "grievous Wolves"

> Who all the sacred mysteries of Heav'n
> To thir own vile advantages shall turn
> Of lucre and ambition, and the truth
> With superstitions and traditions taint.
>
> [12. 508–12]

God's faithful remnant, whose action is symbolized by an Enoch or Noah, are the seed of the entire race's future regeneration. Though Thomas Greene is surely justified in arguing that, in its strong suggestion of internalized action and of a heroism which is detachable from the community, *Paradise Lost* contributed to the destruction of the epic,[29] we must note that Milton's conception of epic *Virtus* is still essentially public and communal. Like Plato's *politici*, Milton's just men are re-orderers of reality, who anatomize false doctrine and proclaim or "denounce" the truth. Enoch is

> The only righteous in a World perverse,
> And therefore hated, therefore so beset
> With Foes for daring single to be just,
> And utter odious Truth.
>
> [11. 701–04]

Noah is of the same famous pattern:

> fearless of reproach and scorn,
> Or violence, hee of thir wicked ways
> Shall them admonish, and before them set
> The paths of righteousness, how much more safe,
> And full of peace, denouncing wrath to come
> On thir impenitence.
>
> [11. 811–16]

It does not help a great deal to insist that all the just men in *Paradise Lost* are typologies of Christ, though they are clearly like him in many ways. It is truer to say, I think, that in Milton's poem providential process brings forth by turns, individuated embodiments of degenerated and regenerated mythic configurations. Christ, in fact, differs essentially from Milton's other just men in that he must ultimately put an end to the turning. Like him, however, the others do recreate a bond of true conviction, a renewed covenant, by *denouncing* to man. The Satanic host is therefore right to feel that Abdiel, another just creature, is *preaching* to them. But they are wrong in supposing that he does not *understand* them or that he does not know their "season" (cf. 5. 850 ff.). They fail to appreciate, as do perhaps many modern men, that moralizing or preaching,

29. *The Descent from Heaven,* p. 407.

rightly conceived, is a far more inclusive act than mere imagining. All of Milton's just men are preachers. More and more we are given to understand that the myth of the bruising seed itself concerns an act of preaching. When Adam coaxes Michael to "say where and when" the great event is to take place, the angel forces him, with a measure of contempt, to abandon his debased imaginings for higher understanding:

> Dream not of thir fight,
> As of a Duel, or the local wounds
> Of head or heel: not therefore joins the Son
> Manhood to Godhead, with more strength to foil
> Thy enemy; nor so is overcome
> *Satan,* whose fall from Heav'n, a deadlier bruise,
> Disabl'd not to give thee thy death's wound:
> Which hee, who comes thy Saviour, shall recure,
> Not by destroying *Satan,* but his works
> In thee and in thy Seed: nor can this be,
> But by fulfilling that which thou didst want,
> Obedience to the Law of God . . .
>
> . . . .
> Proclaiming Life to all who shall believe
> In his redemption.
>
> [12. 386–408]

In the discipline of approaching God's covenant, with its culminating mystery of proclaimed redemption, the crude form of the seed myth must be radically revised, much as is the myth of epic heroism. The demise of Adam's violent conception of the myth is itself part of the cure and part of the proclamation. Here it is useful to recall Gerhard Friedrich's account of the historical Christian keryx: "the true preacher is God or Christ Himself. . . . The decisive thing is the action, the proclamation itself. . . . The divine intervention takes place through the proclamation [which] does not announce that something will happen." God's "proclamation is itself event. . . . The [*kerygma*] is the mode in which the divine Logos comes to us." [30]

30. *Theological Dictionary of the New Testament,* ed. Gerhard Kittel, trans. Geoffrey W. Bromiley (Grand Rapids, Mich., 1965), 3 : 688–716.

As the poem draws to a close, we may be deceived into be-lieving that the myth of the fruit and seed with which it be-gan has become nonmythic if we do not understand the mythic content of the proclamation itself. Milton collects, amplifies, and moderates the demythological procedures Christian theo-logians habitually applied to Judaism in moving from the Old Testament to the New, the Old Law to the New. The Judaic seed-covenant becomes a spirit within all men, com-municated in the proclamation:

> Not only to the Sons of *Abraham's* Loins
> Salvation shall be Preacht, but to the Sons
> Of *Abraham's* Faith wherever through the world;
> So in his seed all Nations shall be blest.
> ·
>   . . . from Heav'n
> Hee [Christ] to his own a Comforter will send,
> The promise of the Father, who shall dwell
> His Spirit within them, and the Law of Faith
> Working through love, upon thir hearts shall write.
>   [12. 447–89]

It is significant that in these lines Milton is building upon Jeremiah's doctrine of demythology—the doctrine first pre-sented, as we saw, in the Old Testament and echoed, almost word for word, in the New:

> Behold, the days come, saith the Lord, that I will make a new covenant with the house of Israel, and with the house of Judah: . . . After those days, saith the Lord, I will put my law in their inward parts, and write it in their hearts; and will be their God, and they shall be my people.

In *Paradise Lost,* substantially as in Calvin's reading of Jere-miah, the Old Law and the Old Covenant are not abolished wholesale; they are renewed and reembodied. In Milton's poem there is no sense of a sharp break between the two cove-nants. One major poetic effect of the seed myth as Milton uses it, is to engender an imaginative continuity between the old and the new. Some readers of Milton's *De Doctrina Christiana* have projected a Milton of severe mood—one who could say, "on the introduction of the gospel, or new covenant through faith in Christ, the whole of the preceding covenant, in other words, the entire Mosaic Law, was abolished"—onto a poetic Milton who was writing in a great kerygmatic tradition of spiritual and imaginative conservation. Milton's epic, notes B. Rajan, "nowhere asserts that the whole Mosaic Law is abolished by the Gospel." This is the case, we should add, not because, as Rajan feels, Milton had "decided that discretion is more poetic than valour," [31] but because abrogation of this kind would have canceled one of the supreme poetic-religious truths that Milton as poet had learned. One major effect of *Paradise Lost* (which is itself, we cannot forget, a recounting of part of the Mosaic Law) is to rescue the Law from hypocrisy and idolatry and to renew it in a faith of poetry and love. Christ's crucifixion, Milton explains, thwarted the attempt to use the Law—which was created *for* man—"against" man (cf. 12. 413–16). Like Calvin, Milton repeatedly emphasizes the perdurable bond of Abraham's ancient covenant.

It was Milton's hope that his poem would soar above the Aonian mount and stand with the divine muse, the muse "that on the secret top / Of Oreb, or of Sinai [did] inspire / That Shepherd, who first taught the chosen Seed" (1. 6–8). The keynote Mosaic parallel is heartfelt and suggestive. Milton was surely aware that even if his epic should succeed in countering the regressive turn against "sacred mysteries" which the "grievous Wolves" had brought about, even if his song should succeed in making its contribution toward regerminating the implanted covenantal seed, the poet himself would not, in any case, survive to see it. The glimpsed "Land / Promis'd to Abraham and his Seed" (12. 260) was not to be Milton's portion. For that fulfillment he must trust in Jesus, as Moses had to rely on Joshua:

31. *The Works of John Milton,* ed. Frank Allen Patterson et al. (New York, 1934), 16 : 113, 125, and 133. Cited and discussed by Rajan, Paradise Lost *and the Seventeenth Century Reader* (Ann Arbor, 1967), pp. 28–29.

> therefore shall not *Moses*, though of God
> Highly belov'd . . . his people into *Canaan* lead;
> But *Joshua* whom the Gentiles *Jesus* call,
> His Name and Office bearing, who shall quell
> The adversary Serpent, and bring back
> Through the world's wilderness long wander'd man
> Safe to eternal Paradise of rest.
>
> [12. 307–14]

We have seen that in Milton's epic the road back to Paradise traces a pattern of replacement. Edenic gardens are won from Hesperian fields, and holy mounts from opprobrious hills. Milton perhaps implies that England itself is the outermost verge of the displaced order. The fable of Saturn, an exiled shadow of divinity, tells how he "Fled over Adria to th' Hesperian Fields, / And o'er the Celtic roam'd the utmost Isles" (1. 520–21), the Celtic land of Britain frequently identified with the Hesperides.[32] Milton's own prophetic hill, the haunt of his muse, is hard to place. It, too, is a locus of displacement, of epic hills rejected and prophetic ones remembered. But in *Paradise Lost* mere physical placement or displacement is of no real importance: "God attributes to place / No sanctity, if none be thither brought / By Men who there frequent, or therein dwell" (11. 836–38). It may be that Milton wished us to understand that England itself—pushed out into the Atlantic—is analogous to the removed *Pisgah* of Paradise, when he had Michael tell us,

> then shall this Mount
> Of Paradise by might of Waves be mov'd
> Out of his place, push'd by the horned flood,
> With all his verdure spoil'd, and Trees adrift
> Down the great River to the op'ning Gulf,
> And there take root an Island salt and bare,
> The haunt of Seals and Orcs, and Sea-mews' clang.
>
> [11. 829–35]

32. See Hughes's note on these lines.

It is possible that for the blind, embittered Milton, England's green and pleasant land had already become, as it was to be in Blake's *Milton,* a dark habitation of Satanic sterility. This is the place of imagination to which Milton brings his own poetic sanctity. There he makes the Sion hill which he visits nightly (cf. 3. 30 ff.). It is there that he rediscovers the covenant enshrined, there that he issues his proclamation.

4

Dryden's Circle of Divine Power

The decades that attended the birth of English Augustan poetry were a period of trauma for the national consciousness, a time of mythologies moving upon the face of the deep. Milton's bituminous lake is only one—an enormous one—of its many steaming pools. That remarkable collection of Restoration verse called *The Poems on Affairs of State* is, in effect, a record of icon-breaking and icon-making.[1] In poems like *A Pulpit to Let* (1665), *Nostradamus' Prophecy* (1672), *A Dialogue between Nathan and Absalom* (1680), or *The Waking Vision* (1681) we find rather pathetic attempts to assume the office of the herald and to proclaim the demise, birth, or resuscitation of temporal and ecclesiastical power.

It was just at this time that the first English Augustan discovered his métier. Dryden's interest in the power of Juvenal's public voice, or "commonwealth genius" as he called it, led him to consider closely the "design" or structure of Juvenalian satire and of classical verse satire in general. Mary Claire Randolph has pointed out that Dryden came to appreciate, as had no English critic before him, the classical satirist's dependence upon "a bi-partite" structure in which "some specific vice or folly, selected for attack, was turned about on all its sides in Part A . . . and its opposing virtue was recommended in Part B."[2] On a specific, auspicious day around the year 1673, this

1. Cf. *Poems on Affairs of State,* ed. George deF. Lord et al., 5 vols. (New Haven, 1963–70), and Ruth Nevo, *The Dial of Virtue: A Study of Poems on Affairs of State in the Seventeenth Century* (Princeton, 1963).

2. "The Structural Design of the Formal Verse Satire," *Philological Quarterly* 21 (1942) : 369.

understanding suddenly crystallized for Dryden into a recognition that his own public poetry must also depend on an organic movement of radical inversion. Twenty years after the fact, his recollection of this intellectual event is still suffused with excitement. We find him now, in 1693, explaining to Dorset the secret of his heroic satire:

> I have given your Lordship but this bare hint, in what verse and in what manner this sort of satire may be best managed. Had I time, I could enlarge on the beautiful turns of words and thoughts; which are requisite in this, as in heroic poetry itself, of which the satire is undoubtedly a species. With these beautiful turns I confess myself to have been unacquainted, till about twenty years ago, in a conversation which I had with that noble wit of Scotland, Sir George Mackenzie. He asked me why I did not imitate in my verses the turns of Mr Waller and Sir John Denham, of which he repeated many to me. . . . Some sprinklings of this kind I had also formerly in my plays; but they were casual, and not designed. But this hint, thus seasonably given me, first made me sensible of my own wants, and brought me afterwards to seek for the supply of them in other English authors. . . . At last I had recourse to . . . Spenser, the author of that immortal poem called the *Fairy Queen;* and there I met with that which I had been looking for so long in vain. . . . Looking farther into the Italian, I found Tasso had done the same; nay more, that all the sonnets in that language are on the turn of the first thought.[3]

Dryden's "turns" are not only or simply tropes; they refer to the kind of structural reversal that takes place, as he indicates, between the octave and sestet of the Petrarchan sonnet. These "turns" of thought, when supplied with a voice of mythic authority and applied to the realm of public myth, yielded him a firm grip on a procedure of mythopoeic displacement. It is no wonder that his major poems of public concern—*Absalom and*

3. *Of Dramatic Poesy and Other Essays,* ed. George Watson (London, 1962), 2 : 149–51.

Achitophel (1681), *The Medall* (1682), *Religio Laici* (1682), and *The Hind and the Panther* (1687)—represent his mastery of this mode. The first two of these poems, and their ambience, are our present concern.

Epilogue Spoken to the King . . . at Oxford . . . 1681

The Popish Plot and the Exclusion Crisis form a distinct chapter of poetic stimulus in Dryden's career. They called into play all his imaginative receptors and led him into creative relation with the throne. This special combination of stimulus and stance was to be decisive in bringing to life one of the greatest satires in any language, *Absalom and Achitophel*. It also confirmed Dryden in the methods that were to serve him throughout his golden decade. This was his moment of ripeness.

In spite of the stories about the royal fiat that created *Absalom and Achitophel*,[4] it is probable that the poem first had a Danaë-like genesis in the downpour of alarm and anger which descended upon (and burst from) most sensitive Englishmen in the early months of 1681. Hysteria over the alleged Roman Catholic conspiracy passed naturally into a passionate attempt to exclude Roman Catholic James from the royal succession and, by corollary, to curtail the powers of Rome-leaning Charles. Though biographers have not yet been able to date with real precision the commencement of Dryden's direct personal involvement in the emergency, the political and literary dates that chiefly concern us are clear enough: Charles dissolved the Oxford parliament on 28 March 1681; on 8 April he ordered the publication of *His Majesties Declaration to all His Loving Subjects Touching the Causes and Reasons that moved Him to Dissolve the Two last Parliaments;* by 22 June Dryden had published his epistolary *His Majesties Declaration Defended; Absalom and Achitophel* was in the booksellers' stalls by 17 November.[5]

4. Cf. Wallace Maurer, "Who Prompted Dryden to Write *Absalom and Achitophel?*" *Philological Quarterly* 40 (1961): 130–38.

5. For historical background see Godfrey Davies, "The Conclusion of Dryden's *Absalom and Achitophel,*" *Huntington Library Quarterly* 10

But we should note that even by mid-March Dryden's imagination was running powerfully in the tracks of the crisis and
of his own imminent creativity. His *Epilogue Spoken to the
King at the opening the Play-House at Oxford on Saturday
last. Being March the Nineteenth 1681*—spoken, we should
add, to a king's company which came to Oxford on armed
alert and to a bevy of blue-ribboned Whig hats flaunting the
motto "No Popery, No Slavery"—is already replete with many
of the most powerful elements of his great public poems. It is
marked by the salubrious self-confidence of a mind that has
managed to encompass, and even in some sense *control*, vast
objects. The *Epilogue* (which replaced an earlier, vaguely por-
nographic one Dryden had written for the same play) [6] may
usefully serve as prologue to *Absalom and Achitophel*, which
is itself, from one point of view, a mirror of the tension and
royal assertion witnessed at Oxford in the days following 19
March. The *Epilogue* is among Dryden's boldest compositions:

> As from a darkn'd Roome some Optick glass
> Transmits the distant Species as they pass;
> The worlds large Landschape is from far descry'd,
> And men contracted on the Paper glide;
> Thus crowded *Oxford* represents Mankind,
> And in these Walls *Great Brittain* seems Confin'd.
> *Oxford* is now the publick *Theater;*
> And you both Audience are, and Actors here.
> The gazing World on the New Scene attend,
> Admire the turns, and wish a prosp'rous end.
> This Place the seat of Peace, the quiet Cell
> Where Arts remov'd from noisy business dwell,
> Shou'd calm your Wills, unite the jarring parts,
> And with a kind Contagion seize your hearts:
> Oh! may its Genius, like soft Musick move,
> And tune you all to Concord and to Love.
> Our Ark that has in Tempests long been tost,

(1946) : 69–82 and Charles E. Ward, *The Life of John Dryden* (Chapel
Hill, 1961), pp. 157 ff.

6. Charles Saunders's *Tamerlane the Great*.

Cou'd never land on so secure a Coast.
From hence you may look back on Civil Rage,
And view the ruines of the former Age.
Here a New World its glories may unfold,
And here be sav'd the remnants of the Old.[7]

Already evident is Dryden's sense of a momentous, pressurized conversion of energy and matter that must somehow eventuate in a recovery of the mysterious equilibrium—the "Genius" of culture and civilization—that is alone capable of insuring man's continued creative existence. The poem itself attempts to exemplify that genius.

In the fifteen years since Dryden's erstwhile colleague "noble Boyle" [8] made known his portable version of the ancient *camera obscura,* the workings of the device had become what might be called a commonplace curiosity. The poem's controlling simile relies on the gradual augmenting of a general half-knowledge to project its image of a darkened, endangered kingdom. Like the *camera,* especially as it had long been used as an aid by painters, the poem contracts, focuses, and composes. It is in these senses, too, that "Oxford represents Mankind": the world is contracted to Great Britain; *Great* Britain is reduced to Oxford; Oxford is poured into its theater; the theater—the chamber or "Roome"—transmits to the paper; and there the artist traces the lines that now appear on the page of verses before us.[9] The act of abstraction and composition symbolized by the "Optick glass" is the function of "Arts remov'd from noisy business" which can unite "jarring parts." Though a couplet like *"Oxford* is now the publick Theater; / And you both Audience are, and Actors here," delicately prods the mind of the auditor, particularly in the half-admonitory "here," to enter the doors of the poet's new world, the poem is not an ontological island. The sense of interaction between

7. Citations from Dryden's poetry are to *The Poems of John Dryden,* ed. James Kinsley, 4 vols. (Oxford, 1958).

8. "To My Honour'd Friend, Dr. Charleton" (1663), l. 27.

9. The *camera* imagined in the poem may be of the cabin variety, in which the entire room where the spectators find themselves is the image chamber.

reality and art, audience and actors, is primary. In fact, the poet invites prince and parliamentarian to participate self-consciously in the idealizing activity of the imagination so that the imagination of the spectator may unite with the form of the actor (or *Epilogue*) and, by so doing, inform the mind of the statesman.

The "New Scene" is the old turned new (cf. l. 10) by the Genius of England and Oxford and laureate poetry. It is itself the remnant saved from the raging flood, crowded into a Noah's ark, an Oxford theater, or a poetic artifact. It safely conveys an ark, also, of covenant—an image of that which cannot change and which is the "distant Species" of which all earthly relation is mere metaphor. When we look "From hence" to see a "New World" rise on "the ruines of the former Age" we are standing with both feet on the magic mountain to whose summit only the myth-displacing poet can conduct us. Without his converting, turning optic glass, his contracting-dilating power, we would indeed all be sitting in a hopelessly darkened room.

We do not know how the hint or request or command to write an appropriate epilogue for 19 March was delivered to Dryden. But we may be certain that he was fully aware of the herald-like office the charge and the occasion entailed. It is tempting to imagine the effect on the audience of the *Epilogue's* (it may also have been the evening's!) climactic exhortation to save "the remnants of the Old": a glitter in the deep, inscrutable royal eyes? Whig upper lips half-curled in detestation? The *Epilogue's* modulated clarion subtly but masterfully exercises a royal mandate. Prepotency is its keynote—from the opening, engulfing, "New World" version of the classical simile to the royally condescending last line, "Be Gods in Senates, but be Mortals here." Individual and vital though it is, the voice of the poet is one with the authority that empowers it, and one with the society for which it stands.

Absalom and Achitophel

Dryden's sense of intimate, depersonalized involvement in communal emergency—perhaps the hallmark of all great pub-

lic poets—grew exponentially in the weeks following the dissolution of parliament. His polemical defense of the *Declaration*
had the effect of visibly numbering him among the audience-
actors in the national drama, the drama that was twice more to
be his poetic subject. True, in his own person he carried little
political weight; but then his poetic voice in *Absalom and
Achitophel* is far more capacious than any private man's. Its
full emergence as a self-conscious entity is postponed in the
poem until it can be counted in the miniscule but overpower-
ing catalog of the king's friends: "my Muse" (l. 854), "my
weary Muse" (l. 898), the "recording Muse" which is among
the kingdom's "Noblest Objects" (ll. 827–28), only makes itself known after we hear,

> Friends he [David] has few, so high the Madness grows,
> Who dare be such, must be the peoples Foes:
> Yet some there were, ev'n in the worst of days;
> Some let me name, and naming is to praise.
>
> [ll. 813–16]

As an active presence, the poet's muse has—as it must have—
both a personal, first person identity and a diffuse, associative
existence as one crucial aspect of the king's corporate person:
Barzillai's large heart, for example, knows to choose the muse
(cf. ll. 826–28); the bishop of "the Western dome" speaks
"heavenly eloquence" (l. 869); detached Amiel was "form'd to
speak a Loyal Nation's Sense" (l. 905); and Jotham (George
Savile) represents a suggestive, impersonal parallel to the
author's own much criticized allegiances:

> *Jotham* of piercing wit and pregnant thought,
> Indew'd by nature, and by learning taught
> To move Assemblies, who but onely try'd
> The worse awhile, then chose the better side;
> Nor chose alone, but turn'd the balance too;
> So much the weight of one brave man can doe.
>
> [ll. 882–87]

David of the "tunefull Harp" (l. 196) is naturally the Muses'
muse; his is the inspiration which is breathed into his poet's

song. It is this relation that will make it possible for the poet
to speak through the king's voice in the climax of the composition.

But all this is not to say that the poet's voice is simply the
monarch's mouthpiece. Far from it. The model for the muse of
Absalom and Achitophel is to be found in Adriel,

> Sharp judging *Adriel* the Muses friend,
> Himself a Muse. . . .
> True to his Prince; but not a Slave of State.
>
> [ll. 877–79]

For some reason many readers have been unwilling to recognize that the poem's opening lines contain unmistakable and
severe criticism of the king himself. Though one part of their
function is, undoubtedly, to raise the issue of illegitimacy upon
which the poem's rejection of Monmouth-Shaftesbury is based,
and another is to erect the mythic scaffolding from which the
narrative is to be constructed, they also make clear that the first
and originating illegitimate act belonged to the king and that
he, in a vital sense, is to blame for the crisis:

> In pious times, e'r Priest-craft did begin,
> Before *Polygamy* was made a sin;
> When man, on many, multiply'd his kind,
> E'r one to one was, cursedly, confind:
> When Nature prompted, and no law deny'd
> Promiscuous use of Concubine and Bride;
> Then, *Israel*'s Monarch, after Heaven's own heart,
> His vigorous warmth did, variously, impart
> To Wives and Slaves: And, wide as his Command,
> Scatter'd his Maker's Image through the Land.

One need hardly strain to see that the surprising word
use—"use of Concubine and Bride"—indicates mere mechani-
cal lust, or that the word *command* implies royal rape. Dryden
was clearly aware that the David allegory carried potential liabilities for Charles's cause. He could have avoided them alto-
gether, but he chose to give them veiled prominence. Biblical
David's use of concubine and bride extended, as we all know,

and as Absalom will remind us (cf. l. 710), to brides other than his own. Even in Uriah's time there obviously was a law that denied this farther reach of promiscuity. The sin is adultery—the biblical metaphor for all inauspicious beginnings—not mere polygamy. In so far as the poem is a prophetic allegory based on the David story, David's anointing prophet, Samuel-Dryden, cannot forbear rebuking that which, in 1681, was its own kind of excessive sexuality. Considering the nature of the crisis, it must have seemed peculiar to Dryden that on 19 March the king should have found it necessary to come to the theater with *two* of his mistresses.

One important effect, then, of the first ten lines is to inform us that though the poem is a royalist satire written in heroic verse, in which the primary subject is the king, the piece is not to be epic panegyric. The opening banter is, in fact, a subtle recusatio in which we and the king are given to understand that, for good and relevant reasons, the poet cannot simply sing the epic hero's victory—present or predicted—over his enemies. Though the poet has dedicated himself to the king's cause, he insists on his independence of judgment and description. The king must understand that it is only in this way that the poet can express and assert the ideal of kingship.

Closely related to this jolting approach to his epic subject is Dryden's audacious subjugation of narrative, a phenomenon that many readers of *Absalom and Achitophel* have found seriously disconcerting.[10] The general problem of truncated fable in heroic satire—a problem frequently remarked by critics of Augustan poems—must be understood in relation to its antecedents in the Enlightenment tradition, which tended to disdain or mistrust the use of fable. Dryden himself openly condemned the "tattling quality of . . . narrative." [11] For all his desire to write a sweeping epic, his poetic practice suggests that he was in principle averse to embodying his pro-

10. For a different approach to the narrative structure of *Absalom and Achitophel*, see Earl Miner, *Dryden's Poetry* (Bloomington, Ind., 1967), pp. 106–43.

11. *Of Dramatic Poesy and Other Essays*, 2 : 85.

foundest ideas in narrative structures.[12] We have hardly begun to assess the significance of this aspect of Dryden's public muse. In *Absalom and Achitophel,* we must begin to see, it manifests itself in a disjunction of narrative and argument that ultimately makes possible a remarkable union of myth and dialectic.

The king described in the opening lines is associated with a form of profligate or promiscuous imagination that is the aesthetic and political anti-ideal of the poem. In fact, the poem furnishes a kind of aesthetic model to enhance our understanding of its formal procedures: Dryden obliquely describes the work as intentionally *scanted.*[13] The sharp contrast between the excuse for rebellion offered by David's son, that he has been "Scanted by a Niggard Birth" (l. 369), and the poet's eulogy of Barzillai's loyal son as a "Narrow Circle, but of Pow'r Divine, / Scanted in Space, but perfect in thy Line!" (ll. 838–39), suggests the opposing intellectual modes presented in the poem. The couplet must ultimately be seen as part of the poem's commentary on its own form: by its own design, it too is scanted in space; it too is a narrow circle, beginning with David and ending with him; and its verse is perfect in its linear (and verse) development toward an ideal of divine power. The poet will not admit into the confines of his art those he considers "Lords, below the Dignity of Verse" (l. 570), even if their presence would pad out the story. "Nor," he insists, "shall the Rascall Rabble here have Place" (l. 579), nor "the rest, who better are forgot" (l. 630). This careful husbanding of poetic energy, time, and space is offered in proximate contrast to the quintessence of the "tattling" mind, Corah-Oates, the "well breath'd Witness of the Plot" (l. 631), whose prophetic utterances "like Visionary flights appear; /

---

12. This was an attitude shared by eighteenth-century Augustans as well: cf. Geoffrey Tillotson, *Augustan Poetic Diction* (London, 1964), p. 134.

13. It is no wonder that Ian Jack, *Augustan Satire: Intention and Idiom in English Poetry, 1660–1750* (Oxford, 1966), pp. 72–73, should find himself using the word *scamped* to describe the narrative parts of *Absalom and Achitophel.* Jack feels that the poem is "more static than dynamic."

The Spirit caught him up," says the poet, "the Lord knows
where" (ll. 656–57).

We should not be surprised to find that the enemy imagination is possessed of substantial poetic gifts. Even the faceless
"Rascall Rabble" are said to be adept and competitive crafts-
men of innovative fantasy:

> The *Solymæan* Rout; well Verst of old,
> In Godly Faction, and in Treason bold;
> Cowring and Quaking at a Conqueror's Sword,
> But Lofty to a Lawfull Prince Restor'd;
> Saw with Disdain an *Ethnick* Plot begun,
> And Scorn'd by *Jebusites* to be Out-done.
>
> [ll. 513–18]

The very first line of the poem suggests that "craft" or artful-
ness is a vital part of the poet's concern. Of course, this craft
is said to be that of the priests, but in *Absalom and Achitophel*
priests means no more than the undifferentiated class of
panderers to spiritual degeneracy who create whatever false
eidolon or golden calf the mob demands. Of the Jews we hear,

> Gods they had tri'd of every shape and size
> That God-smiths could produce, or Priests devise;
>
> [ll. 49–50]

and a similar sentiment is expressed in the Jeremiah-like description of the Jebusite "Gods disgrac'd, and burnt like common wood":

> This set the Heathen Priesthood in a flame;
> For Priests of all Religions are the same:
> Of whatsoe'r descent their Godhead be,
> Stock, Stone, or other homely pedigree,
> In his defence his Servants are as bold
> As if he had been born of beaten gold.
>
> [ll. 97–103]

Dryden uses the priestly image to suggest the mythopoetic,
transubstantiating powers of the purveyors of the Plot:

> that Plot, the Nation's Curse,
> Bad in it self, but represented worse.
> Rais'd in extremes, and in extremes decry'd;
> With Oaths affirm'd, with dying Vows deny'd.
> Not weigh'd, or winnow'd by the Multitude;
> But swallow'd in the Mass, unchew'd and Crude.
>
> [ll. 108–13]

The reader may at first be confused by the fact that Dryden does not differentiate between those who allegedly conspired in the Popish Plot and those who "represent" the plot and use fear of it to political advantage—what we might call the difference between plot-makers and plot-mongers. Dryden intentionally conflates them. The Popish Plot becomes the Whig Plot:

> The Good old Cause reviv'd, a Plot requires.
> Plots, true or false, are necessary things,
> To raise up Common-wealths, and ruin Kings.
>
> [ll. 82–84]

Achitophel is a *maker,* a poet, of the plot as well as its exploiter:

> The wish'd occasion of the Plot he takes,
> Some Circumstances finds, but more he makes.
>
> [ll. 208–09]

Absalom would "Popularly prosecute the Plot" (l. 490) in both senses of the word *prosecute.*

Aesthetically considered, the plot is an overwrought design, conceived from "hudled Notions" and created a "shapeless Lump" (ll. 171–72). It is based, we note, on "Some Truth" (l. 114), on stories of primal perfection imperfectly told; but it is now false. In its essential configuration can be descried both a description and an expression of man's longing for reversal of the conditions of reality and for revolution in the location of authority:

> govern'd by the *Moon,* the giddy *Jews*
> Tread the same track when she the Prime renews:

And once in twenty Years, their Scribes Record,
By natural Instinct they change their Lord.

[ll. 216-19]

The desire to renew the *Prime* cannot be considered evil in itself. *Absalom and Achitophel,* after all, concludes with cosmic renewal—with the beginning of "a Series of new time" (l. 1028). The urgent question is whether the moment of instauration is to herald restored health and creativity— "mighty Years in long Procession" (l. 1029)—or whether the shock of change is to be the signal for inexorable dissipation and decline toward chaos. For Dryden the acid test is a certain imaginative remembrance of the "Lawfull Lord" (l. 1031) who stands behind all man's images of supernal order. Without this fixed image the imagination is seen to become gross and anarchic.

As a work of art whose subject is politics or statesmanship, *Absalom and Achitophel* depends for its unity upon its intense concern with those aspects of the imaginative life which may bring about either the perfection or the ruin of the state: design that can shrink to scheming designs; national myth that can be reduced to plot; craft that can degenerate to craftiness; heavenly eloquence that can metamorphose into Satanic seduction; and great wit that can give way to madness. Achitophel, the "Pilot" (l. 159) of the plot, simultaneously manifests all these forms of degenerated imagination, as when he describes his relation to David:

> To ply him with new Plots, shall be my care,
> Or plunge him deep in some Expensive War;
> Which when his Treasure can no more Supply,
> He must, with the Remains of Kingship, buy.
> His faithful Friends, our Jealousies and Fears,
> Call *Jebusites;* and *Pharaoh*'s Pentioners:
> Whom, when our Fury from his Aid has torn,
> He shall be Naked left to publick Scorn.
> The next Successor, whom I fear and hate,
> My Arts have made Obnoxious to the State;

> Turn'd all his Vertues to his Overthrow,
> And gain'd our Elders to pronounce a Foe.
>
> [ll. 393–404]

In such passages we realize how wide of the mark Dr. Johnson
was firing when he complained that the "original structure of
the poem was defective; allegories drawn to great length will
always break; Charles could not run continually parallel with
David." [14] Dryden was, in fact, presaging in powerful ways,
and for cogent artistic reasons, what Geoffrey Tillotson has
called Johnson's (and Pope's) characteristic slighting of "narrative, that manner of writing in which continuity is broken
as seldom as possible." [15] Achitophel reveals that the plot-
mongers are themselves the original offenders in the cynical
abuse of biblical allegorizing. In their hands it becomes a form
of licentious metaphor, its intellectual content severely at-
tenuated and banally reduced to mere name-calling. The allegory itself tends to become detachable and dispensable; it is
indeed shown to be broken in coherence and false in application. Even the exploitation of Miltonic biblical allegory is
seen to be a Whig stratagem. It is a case of the devil using
scripturelike myth for his own purposes, of plot-monger perversion of sanctified story. Achitophel says of David:

> He is not now, as when on *Jordan*'s Sand
> The Joyfull People throng'd to see him Land,
> Cov'ring the *Beach*, and blackning all the *Strand:*
> But, like the Prince of Angels from his height,
> Comes tumbling downward with diminish'd light;
> Betray'd by one poor Plot to publick Scorn.
>
> [ll. 270–75]

Achitophel's strategy is clear enough. It is to *turn* his royal
enemies' mythlike virtures into antimyths and to bring fear
and tension to a calamitous head so that a thunderous, mythmaking pronouncement of "Foe" may take place. Here and

14. *Lives of the English Poets,* ed. George Birkbeck Hill (Oxford, 1905),
1 : 436–37.
15. *Augustan Poetic Diction,* p. 133.

elsewhere the plot-mongers show acute awareness of the turning, proclamatory possibilities of a free-floating, mythically
chaotic, plot imagination. The malcontent Jews, for example,

> Who banisht *David* did from *Hebron* bring,
> And, with a Generall Shout, proclaim'd him King

are made to wonder

> why, so long, they had obey'd
> An Idoll Monarch which their hands had made:
> Thought they might ruine him they could create;
> Or melt him to that Golden Calf, a State.
>
> [ll. 59–66]

Achitophel takes for himself the office of keryx, to tell Absalom
that his coming is presaged in

> the Sacred Prophets rage:
> The Peoples Prayer, the glad Deviners Theam,
> The Young-mens Vision, and the Old mens Dream!
> . . . .
> Swift, unbespoken Pomps, thy steps proclaim,
> And stammerring Babes are taught to lisp thy Name.
>
> [ll. 237–43]

Corah's testimonies are described in iconic terms because they,
too, represent a specious plot-kerygma and should be associated, the poet notes, not with Moses's serpent of salvation
but with Satan's lies:

> *Corah,* thou shalt from Oblivion pass;
> Erect thy self thou Monumental Brass:
> High as the Serpent of thy mettall made,
> While Nations stand secure beneath thy shade.
>
> [ll. 632–35]

Vigorously ranged against the furor of plot-allegorizing that
reaches its hysterical peak in Corah, is the cold dialectic of the
poet's art—like Adriel's a "Sharp judging" muse (l. 877), like
his "of the Western dome," endowed with "heavenly elo-

quence" tightly clasped to "weighty sense" (ll. 868–69). The poet's dialectic is his ultimate weapon against the plot. It is the elenchus he uses to stop dead the vibrations of fantasizing and to abolish its magical coruscations—as in the last lines in the description of Corah:

> What others in his Evidence did Joyn,
> (The best that could be had for love or coyn,)
> In *Corah*'s own predicament will fall:
> For *witness* is a Common Name to all.
>
> [ll. 678–81]

Division is used to sever and fix that which the plot-mongers strive to "Joyn" and blur: *predicament* is their logical class, *common name* their unalterable identity as individuals within the predicament.[16] They are all no more than paltry men, like Achitophel's son—himself a metaphor for his father's imaginative offspring—an "unfeather'd, two Leg'd thing" (l. 170), a mere man.

Dryden's use in this manner of Plato's *Politicus* definition of man is no accident. Though we need not bother ourselves with questions of direct or indirect influence, it is clear that at its deepest level *Absalom and Achitophel* is conceived, like the *Politicus,* as a dialectical quest for the mythic head of the state. In Achitophel, for example, it is primarily "the Statesman we abhor": we condemn Achitophel's attempt to fill that surpassing office which is far beyond him, though we "praise the Judge" (l. 187). Like many other so-called statesmen, he is only one of a class of "Polititians" (l. 223), inflated bureaucratic servants of the polity or civil government. The description of Zimri's vocation as "Chymist, Fidler, States-man, and Buffoon" (l. 550) is an illogical collocation as significant for *Absalom and Achitophel* as "Puffs, Powders, Patches, Bibles, Billet-doux" is for *The Rape of the Lock.* The task of the true Statesman is in danger of being lost in the shuffle of the Plot. The poem's two catalogs constitute a dialectic of gradual recovery of the divinelike office. When, for example,

16. See *Poems on Affairs of State,* 2 : 481 n.

Achitophel Unites
The Malecontents of all the *Israelites;*
Whose differing Parties he could wisely Joyn,
For several Ends, to serve the same Design,

[ll. 491–94]

the poet conceives his object to be the separation and unraveling of the strands of the knotty "Design," or plot, which
has as its goal the displacing of the monarch with its own compounded entity or its leader's. Straightaway the poet begins
to separate the fibers of the hangman's rope into "Best"
(l. 495), "next" (l. 501), "Others" (l. 505), "Who follow next"
(l. 511), etc. The poet never doubts for a moment the mythic
potency of these instrumentalities en masse, in a body:

Such were the tools; but a whole Hydra more
Remains, of sprouting heads too long, to score.

[ll. 541–42]

Like the *Politicus, Absalom and Achitophel* employs a massive myth, presented in fragmentary form, to complement its
dialectical movement. The true myth, which is the antecedent
of the hotly retailed distortions spread abroad in scriptural
allegorizing (much as the plot is based on "Some Truth"
dimly remembered), must be recovered from the distortions
themselves. Dryden's satiric dismissal of plot-allegorizing
should not mislead us into believing that he really wishes to
eject from his poem all manner and matter of scriptural
parallel. The realization that the poet plays boldly with his
narrative should not inebriate us. A recent critic has leaped
to the mistaken conclusions that in *Absalom and Achitophel*
"Dryden ignores the implications of the scriptural text that he
presumably draws upon," that he intentionally debased scriptural tradition, and that the poem has "no spiritual kinship
with the original ideas of scripture." [17] A much more sober
and imaginative account is offered by Ruth Nevo, who notes
that it was Dryden's "genius to exploit the perception that

17. Leon M. Guilhamet, "Dryden's Debasement of Scripture in *Absalom and Achitophel,*" *Studies in English Literature* 9 (1969) : 395–409.

scripture, while no monopoly of a single class or party, is nevertheless the fundamental well-spring of the epic view of life as it existed in his day in Puritan myth and republican ethos." Dryden's procedure, in this view, consists of turning "the tables upon those who held the key to epic in his day by the appropriation to his scheme of their authoritative myth." [18]

Thus one important function of the poem's dizzying analogizing is to create a parodic stimulus to univocal expression of a more rationally imagined myth. But in the main, the "shapeless Lump" (cf. l. 172) of fragmentary, half-rejected, story is presented as the Silenic housing for the mysterious truth that is to be the poem's proclamation. The entire mass of myth is brought into focus in the poem's methodical treatment of one spectacular example of scripturelike fable, the Miltonic version of Satan's and man's fall presented in *Paradise Lost*. Anne Davidson Ferry has recently argued that "Dryden's uses of *Paradise Lost* in *Absalom and Achitophel* create connections between the epic and the satire as intricate and full of meaning as the literary relationship between any two works in English poetry." Mrs. Ferry attempts to see *Absalom and Achitophel* as "a local, modern instance of Milton's epic," but she is in the end disappointed to find that Dryden fails to follow Milton in building his poem on the "redemptive power" of language and that, therefore, *Absalom and Achitophel* is a sensitive but conspicuous failure.[19] If, in other words, we are to add luster to *Absalom and Achitophel* by pointing to its reliance on *Paradise Lost*, we must have the honesty to admit that, by comparison and in relation to *Paradise Lost*, *Absalom and Achitophel* is a microscopic achievement, and a failed one at that. We must be grateful to

18. *The Dial of Virtue*, pp. 248–50.

19. *Milton and the Miltonic Dryden* (Cambridge, Mass., 1968), pp. 125, 121, and 114. To a certain extent I have oversimplified Mrs. Ferry's argument concerning *Absalom and Achitophel*, but this is its essential logic; and it is, we should note, a logic that has been incubating in Dryden studies for some time. See, for example, Bernard N. Schilling, *Dryden and the Conservative Myth: A Reading of* Absalom and Achitophel (New Haven, 1961), pp. 197 ff.

Mrs. Ferry for recognizing (even while she pursues her fore-gone conclusion that *Absalom and Achitophel* is "a kind of re-enactment of Milton's epic") that, in opposition to *Paradise Lost,* Dryden's satire is

> a vehement denial of pastoral attitudes, here denounced as irresponsible fantasies. . . . Those portions of *Paradise Lost* which recreate Milton's imagining of the original state of innocence were unavailable to Dryden except as targets for the kind of anti-pastoral criticism that informs his presentation of the "Natural" state of man. . . . From the opening lines he warns us that some of our associa-tions for Miltonic language are false, that the Biblical and pastoral notions of an ideal state of nature out of which Milton created his image of unfallen innocence can be dangerously misleading.[20]

But having said all this, it is difficult to understand how one can still believe that, as "a form of literary adaptation, Dry-den's ironic parodies do not intend disparagement of Milton's poem." [21] We can continue to love Brutus without blinding ourselves to the violent way he chooses to glorify Caesar.

One could hardly have expected that the relation of *Absa-lom and Achitophel* to *Paradise Lost* would be unperplexed. *Absalom and Achitophel* is a pointedly anti-Whig, anti-Puritan satire. Milton was not, in himself, an ideal to the Tory Augustans. They could too easily taste in him a danger-ous concoction of all the Whig evils threatening their world. Dryden was, perhaps, noting a poetic manifestation of Milton's unruly biases when he remarked of *Paradise Lost* (long before Blake) that "the Devil [is] his hero, instead of Adam." [22] Johnson's veneration for Milton the poet was too great to countenance such a suggestion, but his account of Milton's politics bears a disquieting resemblance to Milton's own de-scriptions of the devil:

20. *Milton and the Miltonic Dryden,* pp. 12, 88, 92, and 111.
21. Ibid., p. 32.
22. *Of Dramatic Poesy and Other Essays,* 2 : 233.

Milton's republicanism was, I am afraid, founded in an envious hatred of greatness, and a sullen desire of independence; in petulance impatient of controul, and pride disdainful of superiority. He hated monarchs in the State, and prelates in the Church; for he hated all whom he was required to obey. It is to be suspected that his predominant desire was to destroy rather than establish, and that he felt not so much the love of liberty as repugnance to authority.[23]

Dryden was among the first Englishmen to realize that *Paradise Lost* was, as he had put it in 1677, "undoubtedly one of the greatest, most noble, and most sublime poems which either this age or nation has produced." [24] But in 1681, just seven years after Milton's death, it is hard to imagine that he could have regarded as wholly nonpartisan any product of Milton's redoubtable, Puritan, republican, king-killer pen. Dryden's deliberate choice of Milton's Restoration lament for paradise lost to supply the massive myth of his Tory poem was one of the boldest poetic decisions of his career. Milton was indeed Dryden's angel in *Absalom and Achitophel,* but he was also his wrestling partner. We may speculate that, in making Milton his choice, Dryden was, in part, struggling to adapt to his strongest convictions a structure of belief and feeling to which he had once been—as the whole world knew —personally sympathetic though never really devoted.[25]

By way of amplifying Dr. Johnson's criticism that *Absalom and Achitophel* suffers from an "unpleasing disproportion between the beginning and the end," [26] Arthur W. Hoffman has commented that

the phase of the epic action adumbrated in the [first] section of the poem is truncated; there is a Fall, but the consequences to Adam and to Eden are suspended. At

23. *Lives of the English Poets,* 1 : 157.
24. *Of Dramatic Poesy and Other Essays,* 1 : 196.
25. In 1681 Dryden's enemies circulated a broadsheet of his "Heroique Stanzas" to the memory of Cromwell.
26. *Lives of the English Poets,* 1 : 437.

the point of truncation a second phase of the epic action
is adumbrated, the rout of Satan and his hosts by God.
It may be that Dryden should be censured for cramming
the frame of an "epic in miniature" with two phases of an
epic action which, in their new context and arrangement,
will not submit to a neat joint.[27]

In considering the controlled design of Dryden's dialectical
art, we have come to realize that the lack of "a neat joint"
of this kind is itself probably the passageway to profound
meaning. Indeed, on closer inspection we find that it is itself
the *callida junctura* around which the entire artistry of *Absalom and Achitophel* is organized.

In *Absalom and Achitophel* Dryden's imagination engaged
Paradise Lost under two headings of myth: one, the story of
Edenic innocence, temptation, and fall; the other, God's and
man's revenge on Satan and the restoration of man's covenant
with God. In recounting Achitophel's seduction of Absalom
and of the Jews, Dryden deliberately truncated and mangled a
narrative heavily fraught with mythic implications. The poem
does indeed offer a "vehement denial of pastoral attitudes."
Dryden undoubtedly believed that in the brain of every revo-
lutionary there is lodged a dangerous Edenic fantasy, expressed sometimes as primitivism, sometimes as apocalyptic
millenialism:

> These *Adam*-wits, too fortunately free,
> Began to dream they wanted libertie;
> And when no rule, no president was found
> Of men, by Laws less circumscrib'd and bound,
> They led their wild desires to Woods and Caves,
> And thought that all but Savages were Slaves.
>
> [ll. 51–56]

But it is not accurate to say that there "is in *Absalom and
Achitophel* no Eden from which we have strayed, no natural
innocence we have corrupted. There is therefore in Dryden's
satiric view no Fall of man, no ideal of original purity with

27. *John Dryden's Imagery* (Gainesville, Fla., 1962), pp. 89–90.

which viciousness is contrasted." [28] What *is* true, I think, is that *Absalom and Achitophel* enforces the reader's recognition that, so far as human agency is concerned, human life has changed irrevocably since the Fall. In Dryden's view, we must never imagine that we can return to Eden, although other avenues of divinelike action are still open to us.

Dryden attacks the designing mind, the arbitrary imagination that contrives an abstract model and proceeds to lop off inconvenient segments of reality; and yet he never loses faith that the demands of the projector imagination may be met by recovering the divine design inherent in man's cultural inheritance. One must not lose sight of the highly active mythic state of the poem—which subsists within its satiric myth-destruction—a state constantly moving toward definition and proclamation. One major function of the poem's allegorical form is to suggest from the very first verse the emergence of a pattern of historical replication: the temporal interval of the poem is to give way to "a Series of new time"—or what mythographers refer to as a cosmogonal period of "strong time." [29] *Absalom and Achitophel* is conceived on the assumption that historical process is cyclical, that energies and events build to a peak of tension which can no longer be contained. At such a fateful instant, there are only two alternatives, chaos or proclamation—the dissolution of all moral consciousness or the resurrection of order.

The myth of Satanic evil dies a very special death: it is desiccated by ironic rays of rationality. As Martin Price observes, "Dryden colors the tragic fall of Absalom with an element of fatuity. In *Paradise Lost* Satan's original fall is left mysterious, and his temptation of others is given only in fragments of impressive eloquence. But Dryden collapses the process into a scene whose transparency and brevity make Absalom an object of satire." [30] The sentimentality of regicide

28. *Milton and the Miltonic Dryden*, p. 89.

29. Mircea Eliade, *Myth and Reality*, trans. Willard R. Trask (New York, 1963), p. 34.

30. *To the Palace of Wisdom: Studies in Order and Energy from Dryden to Blake* (New York, 1964), p. 59. Price, pp. 28–78, offers an extremely helpful account of Dryden's dialectical art.

and the romance of revolution are discarded. In rejecting Whiggish myths of pastoral perfectionism, Dryden was operating surgically upon *Paradise Lost.* In the words of one contemporary reader of *Absalom and Achitophel,* it was "As if a Milton from the dead arose, / Filed off the rust, and the right party chose." [31] In refining Milton's ore, Dryden probably felt that he was bringing to light tendencies already powerfully present in *Paradise Lost.*

As an appreciative reader of Milton's masterpiece, and with his special sensitivity in such matters, Dryden was no doubt keenly aware of the epic's own myth-displacing movement, particularly in its conversion of the seed image we examined earlier. In *Absalom and Achitophel,* the destruction of *Paradise Lost's* pastoral myth gives way to an organically related reassertion of the epic's myth of covenantal renewal. David has dispersed his "Maker's Image" to the wind (l. 10). His seed cannot carry "True Succession" (l. 16), though he vainly deludes himself into believing that he sees "His Youthfull Image if his Son renew'd" (l. 32). Achitophel is himself "Noble seed," but he is choked by "Cockle" and "rankness" (ll. 194–95). The tragic fact is that David's seed cannot produce his royal heir. And yet the forbidden gathering of the "Golden fruit" (l. 202) does somehow call forth the germ of lawful continuity. In passing from the first, rejected phase of his Miltonic myth to the second highly honored, reenacted one, Dryden repeats Milton's conversion of the seed myth into a myth of a faithful remnant—"a small but faithful Band" (l. 914) —and of the reappearing "one just man," in this case the "one brave man" who dares to *turn* assemblies toward the king (ll. 884–87).[32] What makes possible this leap between the two phases of myth is a meshing constituent that is also the remedy for the poem's seeming lack of jointure between fable and argument, myth and dialectic. It is the uniquely defined voice of the poet, dialectical, mythic, proclamatory. Like the recurrent "one brave man," he too—indeed, he preeminently, in

31. *The Works of John Dryden,* ed. Sir Walter Scott and George Saintsbury (Edinburgh, 1884), 9 : 215.

32. Barbara Lewalski, "The Scope and Function of Biblical Allusion in *Absalom and Achitophel,*" *ELN* 3 (1965) : 34, has remarked that Dry-

the world of the poem—has been chosen "to speak a Loyal Nation's Sense" (l. 905).

In ways similar to the final solution offered in the *Politicus,* it is the king's or statesman's orator who exercises for him the talismanic power to restore the bond of true conviction. Dr. Johnson has left us the following often quoted criticism of the poem's conclusion:

> Who can forbear to think of an enchanted castle, with a wide moat and lofty battlements, walls of marble and gates of brass, which vanishes at once into air when the destined knight blows his horn before it? [33]

The choice of figure, for all its beauty, is unfortunate. For the divine figure of David was, in fact, meant to carry with it the giant-killer dimension presented in the biblical story. The mature David has not forgotten the use of his destined slingshot, though now it has grown abstract and verbal. When "God-like David" speaks after "long revolving, in his carefull Breast, / Th' event of things" (ll. 934–37), we are offered a clear image of the poem's larger pattern of vicious cycle linearly directed. In the very same image, the poem's structural ideal—a "Narrow Circle . . . of Pow'r Divine, / Scanted in Space, but perfect in . . . Line"—reaches its destined completion. The slingshot is aimed directly at the brain of the evil giant who has "turn'd the Plot to Ruine Church and State" (l. 930). Circular logic, David tells us, must be put right and directed; the aesthetic design must conform to dialectic:

> That one was made for many, they contend:
> But 'tis to Rule, for that's a Monarch's End.
>
> [ll. 945–46]
>
> The Law shall still direct my peacefull Sway,
> And the same Law teach Rebels to Obey:

---

den's catalogs function "like Milton's historical summary in Books XI and XII of *Paradise Lost,* in that both suggest a transformed epic battle continued through the ages." In this qualified sense, Mrs. Ferry is justified in calling *Absalom and Achitophel* a "re-enactment" of *Paradise Lost.*

33. *Lives of the English Poets,* 1 : 437.

> Votes shall no more Establish'd Pow'r controul,
> Such Votes as make a Part exceed the Whole.
>
> [ll. 991–94]

The tarnished "Maker's Image" is refurbished when David's "Train their Maker in their Master hear" (l. 938). Immanence is stressed because the chastened David, who speaks his "Fury," (l. 1005) or furor, is "forc'd, like Heaven, against [his] mind" (l. 1000). The king is transformed; an internal power is revealed and becomes primary in him. The myth of divine law is of itself opened and proclaimed:

> Law they require, let Law then shew her Face;
> They could not be content to look on Grace,
> Her hinder parts, but with a daring Eye
> To tempt the terror of her Front, and Dye.
>
> [ll. 1006–09]

The myth of God's self-revelation merges with the myth of revenge on the serpent and his cohorts: "Viper-like their Mother Plot they tear" (l. 1013). In this high-arching mythic renewal much more than the king is restored. The poet's last line, proclaiming the king's authority—"And willing Nations knew their Lawfull Lord"—is creatively double: the lawful lord is not simply David; the willing nations are part of the Old Testament prophecy of the world's ultimate recognition of the Lord's truth. The poem ends, therefore, not merely with the shoring up of the king's power, but with the reenstatement of the divine presence which makes that power meaningful. This is the consciousness—the knowledge or cognition—which is prior even to the kingly myth, which is, indeed, the myth behind all myths, and which always abides, waiting to be discovered.

The Medall

Dryden's *Medall* is a dazzling performance. Of all his public poems, its conception is perhaps the most unified. But its simplified use of the complex procedures of *Absalom and Achitophel* suggests that Dryden, intent on repeating the success

of the first poem, self-consciously condensed his proven methods and reproduced them, almost according to rule and for-
mula, in the second.

The occasion of the poem played directly into his poetic
hands. To the consternation of the king, Shaftesbury was ac-
quitted of the charge of treason by a packed Whig jury.
Shaftesbury's followers seized on the occasion to issue a medal
commemorating his triumph. Dryden recognized in the medal
an attempt to proclaim a false myth, or "Idol" (l. 7), of
Shaftesburian authority. In the poem, he proceeds by anatomizing the thriving myth into constituent limbs and showing
the body to be merely mortal:

> So like the Man; so golden to the sight,
> So base within, so counterfeit and light.
> One side is fill'd with Title and with Face;
> And, lest the King shou'd want a regal Place,
> On the reverse, a Tow'r the Town surveys;
> O'er which our mounting Sun his beams displays.
>
> [ll. 8–13]

It is a papier-mâché myth, the poet insists, little better and
perhaps much worse than any other man could make: see how
easily it crumples. It is artificial in the bad sense, for in it,
Dryden tells us at line 6, "Art" does not flow from "Nature,"
but rather strives against it. In the ensuing comparison of the
medal and its pretentious inscription with the divine proclamation of the Psalmist, and more important, with the creating
Logos of God—the *act* that first created proud man—Dryden
wittily demolishes the false proclamation of Shaftesbury, as it
was issued by a sheriff of London, Slingsby Bethel:

> The Word, pronounc'd aloud by Shrieval voice,
> *Lætamur,* which, in *Polish,* is *rejoyce.*
> The Day, Month, Year, to the great Act are join'd:
> And a new Canting Holiday design'd.
> Five daies he sate, for every cast and look;
> Four more than God to finish *Adam* took.
>
> [ll. 14–19]

The poet's effort to pierce this false gospel becomes explicit a dozen lines later:

> Bart'ring his venal wit for sums of gold
> He cast himself into the Saint-like mould;
> . . . .
> But, as 'tis hard to cheat a Juggler's Eyes,
> His open lewdness he cou'd ne'er disguise.
> There split the Saint: for Hypocritique Zeal
> Allows no Sins but those it can conceal.
>
> [ll. 32–39]

The poet points us clearly to the fact that the propagation of the false myths (which threaten to supplant the old) is the real danger of Shaftesbury. The medal is therefore symbolic of Shaftesbury's entire program of false mythology proclaimed by a specious keryx in preachments and alarmist cries:

> He preaches to the Crowd, that Pow'r is lent,
> But not convey'd to Kingly Government;
> That Claimes successive bear no binding force;
> That Coronation Oaths are things of course;
> Maintains the Multitude can never err;
> And sets the People in the Papal Chair.
>
> [ll. 82–87]

> The common Cry is ev'n Religion's Test;
> The *Turk's* is, at *Constantinople,* best;
> Idols in *India,* Popery at *Rome;*
> And our own Worship onely true at home.
> . . . .
> This side to day, and that to morrow burns;
> So all are God-a'mighties in their turns.
>
> [ll. 103–10]

It is the "turns" of mythological assumptions, the myth-dis-placing exploitation that has the power of divinization—and that Dryden himself will soon be using for his own purposes—which he works to upset at this point.

In a single brilliant couplet, he lays bare the secret workings of demythological power. Our fathers, he says,

> to destroy the seeds of Civil War,
> Inherent right in Monarchs did declare.
>
> [ll. 113–14]

The declaration of authority that ended the war was made possible by a fragile conversion of the energies and national beliefs involved in the civil war to a fiat of germinal or "inherent" power in the king. Shaftesbury would reverse this delicate achievement. The pseudo-divine medal his followers engrave, "their Conquest to record, / The Stamp and Coyn of their adopted Lord" (ll. 143–44), can only be issued by invading and appropriating the magic circle of kingship symbolized by the royal portrait on the national currency. Their effort is

> Perhaps not wholly to melt down the King;
> But clip his regal Rights within the Ring.
> From thence, t'assume the pow'r of Peace and War.
>
> [ll. 228–30]

The power of these false heralds, the poet notes, is formidable because they seize the proclamatory authority of the Bible itself:

> Happy who can this talking Trumpet seize;
> They make it speak whatever Sense they please!
> 'Twas fram'd, at first, our Oracle t'enquire;
> But, since our Sects in prophecy grow higher,
> The Text inspires not them; but they the Text inspire.
>
> [ll. 162–66]

"Venom" (l. 265), Dryden tells Shaftesbury,

> swells the Breasts
> Of all thy bellowing Renegado Priests,
> That preach up Thee for God.
>
> [ll. 267–69]

The harmful proclamations of these illegitimate heralds must lead to chaos unless, the poet suggests, they can themselves be reversed. In order to effect this reversal, he conducts

the climax and conclusion of his poem in the form of a discursive prophecy in which anatomizing logos and fusing
mythos become inseparable:

> Without a Vision Poets can fore-show
> What all but Fools, by common Sense may know:
>
> . . . .
> The swelling Poyson of the sev'ral Sects,
> Which wanting vent, the Nations Health infects
> Shall burst its Bag; and fighting out their way
> The various Venoms on each other prey.
>
> . . . .
> . . . Frogs and Toads, and all the Tadpole Train
> Will croak to Heav'n for help. . . .
> The Cut-throat Sword and clamorous Gown shall jar,
> In shareing their ill-gotten Spoiles of War:
>
> . . . .
> Their Gen'ral either shall his Trust betray,
> And force the Crowd to Arbitrary sway;
> Or they suspecting his ambitious Aym,
> In hate of Kings shall cast anew the Frame.
>
> [ll. 287–316]

The cycle of melting down existing mythic orders and casting
new medals of falsely constituted power must stop. The poet
has offered a logical analogy between the danger Shaftesbury
represents and the threat of Cromwell that gave way to the
restoration moment, which itself converted the seeds of civil
war into the announcement of inherent monarchical right. By
these means he can now reduce the present situation to the
past and, in the closing lines of the poem, proclaim the future authority of the king:

> Thus inborn Broyles the Factions wou'd ingage;
> Or Wars of Exil'd Heirs, or Foreign Rage,
> Till halting Vengeance overtook our Age:
> And our wild Labours, wearied into Rest,
> Reclin'd us on a rightfull Monarch's Breast.[34]
>
> [ll. 318–22]

34. For commentary on other aspects of the poem, see Alan H. Roper,
Dryden's Poetic Kingdoms (London, 1965), pp. 87–103, and A. E. Wallace

It is a powerful vision, but far more limited than the one achieved in *Absalom and Achitophel,* perhaps because *The Medall* lacks foundation in a commodious myth. For statements of communal truth on the scale of *Absalom and Achitophel,* one would have to go to *Religio Laici* (1682) or *The Hind and the Panther* (1687), religious poems which indicate that after 1681 Dryden came to feel he could speak most effectively by telescoping the awesome distance between him and the authority of his "Lawfull Lord." [35]

Maurer, "The Design of Dryden's *The Medall," Papers on Language and Literature* 2 (1966) : 293–304.

35. In *Dryden and the Abyss of Light: A Study of* Religio Laici *and* The Hind and the Panther (New Haven, 1970), I have discussed in some detail the dialectical and displacemental means Dryden employed in *Religio Laici* to create a ratiocinative "Sun of Righteousness" and in *The Hind and the Panther* to reaffirm Roman Catholic iconic worship in a prophecy of inevitable English reconversion to true faith. Horace's *Epistles,* Dryden announced, served him as a model in composing *Religio Laici,* the first half of his venture in divine maieutics. It is perhaps no accident that the spiritual center of *Religio Laici* is inhabited by those who "follow'd *Reasons* Dictates right" and who "With *Socrates* may see their Maker's Face" (ll. 208–10).

5

Pope and the Hidden God

In Alexander Pope, the young man of twenty-four, we can see immortalizing longings of the same kerygmatic type that gripped Dryden. The "Advertisement" to Pope's *Messiah* (1712) clearly describes his desire to invoke the heraldic powers of both Augustan Rome and biblical Jerusalem. His inspiration came, he tells us, from "reading several passages of the Prophet *Isaiah,* which foretell the coming of Christ and the felicities attending it," and then observing "a remarkable parity between many of the thoughts, and those in the *Pollio* of *Virgil.*" [1] The poem, which is indeed a blend of Isaiah and Virgil, constitutes a fleshless but spirited exercise in the reconstructive paradigm of proclamatory verse:

> The Seas shall waste; the Skies in Smoke decay;
> Rocks fall to Dust, and Mountains melt away;
> But fix'd *His* Word, *His* saving Pow'r remains:
> Thy *Realm* for ever lasts! thy own *Messiah* reigns!
>
> [ll. 105–08]

Windsor-Forest

But Pope's access to a mandate for public proclamation was severely limited.[2] In the opening of *Windsor-Forest* (1713) we

1. Citations from Pope's works are to *The Twickenham Edition of the Poems of Alexander Pope,* ed. John Butt et al. (New Haven, 1939–69), hereafter referred to as *TE.* The "Advertisement" first appeared in 1717.

2. In *The Garden and the City: Retirement and Politics in the Later Poetry of Pope, 1731–1743* (Toronto, 1969), Maynard Mack has explained how the Pope of the 1730s "drew about him publicly [the] almost seamless

observe a poet embarked on a graceful but somewhat desperate
circumnavigation toward the harbor of regal authority:

> Thy forests, *Windsor!* and thy green Retreats,
> At once the Monarch's and the Muse's Seats,
> Invite my Lays. Be present, Sylvan Maids!
> Unlock your Springs, and open all your Shades.
> *Granville* commands: Your Aid O Muses bring!
> What Muse for *Granville* can refuse to sing?

The forest represents a point of incorporation where poet and
monarch have traditionally been located together. But Pope's
muse cannot possibly pretend to any proximate affiliation with
the queen. Instead he finds his access to Anne's investitive com-
mands through Granville, who is quickly named twice and
whom the queen had just created one of twelve new peers who
made possible the Peace of Utrecht, itself the occasion of the
poem's publication. Granville thus becomes more than a metaphor for the monarch. In the poem, he is her surrogate.

When the poet speaks "for" Granville, he not only grants a
request; he also speaks through the peer's own mind and voice
and, by suggestion, through the mind and voice of the monarch
(in somewhat the same way Dryden did for Charles II near the
close of *Absalom and Achitophel*). It is this system of subrogation that gives Pope's poem authority. The same procedure, in
reverse, is used at the end, to depart the poem and to seal its
public integrity—in effect, to dislocate it from any mere private authorship. The poet draws in the reins of his inspired
muse:

> Here cease thy Flight, nor with unhallow'd Lays
> Touch the fair Fame of *Albion*'s Golden Days.
> The Thoughts of Gods let *Granville*'s Verse recite,
> And bring the Scenes of opening Fate to Light.

---

garment formed of ancient Rome and Twickenham and seventeenth-
century retirement precedents, which signalized the posture of the
honest satirist protesting a corrupt society" (p. 193). My discussion
throughout this chapter is heavily indebted to Mack's study.

My humble Muse, in unambitious Strains,
Paints the green Forests and the flow'ry Plains.

[ll. 423–28]

The distinction between hallow'd flight and unambitious
strains is not flattering fiction. It points to the magic circle of
public poetry in which poet and monarch can only conjure
jointly. In important ways the poem itself has been Granville's
verse; and Granville, in turn, recites the thoughts of gods—
kings, "our earthly Gods" (l. 230). In Granville's echoing words
(perhaps most concretely in his participation in the talks that
negotiated the peace) we see the word become action. His
words help bring fate to fruition, in addition to making the
fateful effects known. In this, he and the poet reenact the god-
like creativity of the monarch who had decided to end the chaotic "Series of Intestine Wars" (l. 325):

At length great ANNA said—Let Discord cease!
She said, the World obey'd, and all was *Peace!*

[ll. 327–28]

In Granville, himself a muse represented by a muse, the lines
of force of "earthly Gods" and "God-like Poets" (l. 270) are
brought together. Through him the implicit promise of the
poem's opening couplet—to relocate in Windsor's green retreats the monarch's near the muse's seats—can be fulfilled:

'Tis yours, my Lord, to bless our soft Retreats,
And call the Muses to their ancient Seats.

[ll. 283–84]

In Granville we find compacted an avatar of the poet-statesman-
king.

The methods of subrogation that make all this possible are
themselves modulations of a larger principle of displacement
which receives more extensive application in the poem's theme
of violence sublimated. In Pope's ultimate vision of the Golden
Age, we recall, there is no Edenic immunity to discord. Dangerous energies are only imprisoned and directed to higher
ends:

> The shady Empire shall retain no Trace
> Of War or Blood, but in the Sylvan Chace,
> The Trumpets sleep, while chearful Horns are blown,
> And Arms employ'd on Birds and Beasts alone.
> . . . .
> Behold! *Augusta*'s glitt'ring Spires increase,
> And Temples rise, the beauteous Works of Peace.
>
> [ll. 371–78]

> In Brazen Bonds shall barb'rous *Discord* dwell:
> Gigantick *Pride,* pale *Terror,* gloomy *Care,*
> And mad *Ambition,* shall attend her there.
> . . . .
> There *Faction* roar, *Rebellion* bite her Chain,
> And gasping Furies thirst for Blood in vain.
>
> [ll. 414–22]

This is how Albion's Golden Days are ushered in. The principle of displacement, writ little and writ large, controls and explains a good deal that is happening in *Windsor-Forest,* and it may ultimately help us to reach the unlocked spring or deepest meaning of the poem.

The oaks of Windsor Forest, for example, serve in the poem as a vehicle of removal and, at the same time, absorption, of poetical trans-portation. Early on we hear,

> Let *India* boast her Plants, nor envy we
> The weeping Amber or the balmy Tree,
> While by our Oaks the precious Loads are born,
> And Realms commanded which those Trees adorn.
>
> [ll. 29–32]

And later, Father Thames informs the forest that it is only by being themselves displaced that her oaks can fulfill their charge:

> Thy Trees, fair *Windsor!* now shall leave their Woods,
> And half thy Forests rush into my Floods,
> Bear *Britain*'s Thunder, and her Cross display,

To the bright Regions of the rising Day;

. . . .

For me the Balm shall bleed, and Amber flow,
The Coral redden, and the Ruby glow.

[ll. 385–94]

It is no small mark of Pope's intensely decorous art that the
image of the oaks here elaborated is itself borrowed, or, more
precisely, displaced, from a Golden Age vision—that of Virgil's
Pollio, now revisited—which Pope had come to regard as overstated. The "stubborn oak shall distil dewy honey," Virgil
prophesied, and "every land shall bear all fruits." As Aubrey
Williams has noted, now Pope was only willing to imagine a
Golden Age in which, after the manner of the *Georgics,* peace
and perfection are joined to industry and toil, and in which
Mantua is to be planted with Palestinian palms.[3] One can,
perhaps, never fix with confidence the limits of Pope's allusions, but here we know that we are not merely playing with
words when we say that the displacement capacity of Pope's
oaks is comprised, to a considerable extent, of the displacement, with Virgil's aid, of sanctified Virgilian mythic materials.
Similarly, Pope's vision of a time to come,

when free as Seas or Wind
Unbounded *Thames* shall flow for all Mankind,
Whole Nations enter with each swelling Tyde,
And Seas but joint the Regions they divide;
Earth's distant Ends our Glory shall behold,
And the new World launch forth to seek the Old,

[ll. 397–402]

is itself, as Maynard Mack has noted, a version, "with a difference," of Isaiah's prophesied exaltation of Jerusalem: [4]

the Gentiles shall come to thy light, and kings to the
brightness of thy rising. . . . Then thou shalt see, and

3. See Aubrey Williams, *TE,* 1 : 137 and Mack, *The Garden and the
City,* p. 39.
4. "On Reading Pope," *College English* 7 (1946) : 268.

> flow together, and thine heart shall fear, and be enlarged;
> because the abundance of the sea shall be converted unto
> thee, the forces of the Gentiles shall come unto thee. . . .
> Therefore thy gates shall be open continually.
>
> [Isa. 60 : 3–11]

The difference consists in a redefinition of "the Gentiles" and
in the redirection of the converting sea. In our terms, it represents a displacement of the old Jerusalem by the new and, indeed, of God's Old Testament by his New.

One more example will, I hope, round off our brief survey
of the poem's localized displacement procedures and, at the
same time, lead us back to our discussion of its broader move-
ments. Here I would like to try to extend, in another direction,
Professor Mack's admirable defense of the following much-
maligned couplet: [5]

> See *Pan* with Flocks, with Fruits *Pomona* crown'd,
> Here blushing *Flora* paints th' enamel'd Ground.
>
> [ll. 37–38]

The lines qualify for substantial appreciation along the lines
of our present argument. One detractor, we may recall, sneered
that "Pope would probably have defended these lines by re-
marking that every word in them of any significance . . . is
to be found in descriptive passages of Milton. To which the
answer would be: Precisely so; they are Milton's words and you
have done nothing to make them your own." [6] It is not unlikely that part of Pope's defense (had he cared to make one)
would have been very similar to the words hypothesized for

5. Ibid., pp. 264 ff. For Mack's most recent comments on these lines, see
The Garden and the City, pp. 94–95.

6. Bernard Groom's comment ["Some Kinds of Poetic Diction," *Essays
and Studies by Members of the English Association*, 15 (1929) : 149], cited
and answered by Mack, "On Reading Pope," pp. 264 ff. Don Cameron
Allen, *Mysteriously Meant: The Rediscovery of Pagan Symbolism and Allegorical Interpretation in the Renaissance* (Baltimore, 1970), pp. 292 ff.,
discusses Milton's allusions to Pomona.

him. *Windsor-Forest,* after all, virtually begins with sighing admiration for Milton's *Paradise Lost:*

> The Groves of *Eden,* vanish'd now so long,
> Live in Description, and look green in Song:
> *These,* were my Breast inspir'd with equal Flame,
> Like them in Beauty, should be like in Fame.
>
> [ll. 7–10]

Pope was not trying to keep his emulation a secret. But before we decide that Pope has done nothing to make, say, Pan and Pomona his own, we should consider carefully what Pope (or any other writer going to *Paradise Lost* for literary models) would have observed when he went to see how Milton made Pan and Pomona *his* own.

We are not surprised to find that these two figures, at least, appear in *Paradise Lost* as prime examples of Milton's own displacement techniques. The image of Adam and Eve's abode is lodged in our minds by the devaluation of a pagan mythological one:

> In shadier Bower
> More sacred and sequester'd, though but feign'd,
> *Pan* . . . never slept. . . .
>
> [4.705–07]

> to the Silvan Lodge
> They came, that like *Pomona's* Arbor smil'd
> With flow'rets deck't and fragrant smells; but *Eve*
> Undeckt, save with herself more lovely fair
> Than Wood-Nymph, or the fairest Goddess feign'd.
>
> [5.378–81]

In the same connection Pope would probably not have failed to notice that Milton compares Eve to Flora only once—as she appears to Adam after Satan has infused his dream into her (5.16)—and that the only other time she is compared to Pomona (to be degraded to terms of equality with her) occurs at the climactic moment when Eve, much against Adam's premonition, withdraws her hand from his "like a Wood-Nymph light" (9.386):

> To *Pales,* or *Pomona,* thus adorn'd,
> Likest she seem'd, *Pomona* when she fled
> *Vertumnus,* or to *Ceres* in her Prime,
> Yet Virgin of *Prosperpina* from Jove.
>
> [9.393–96]

In *Paradise Lost,* as we see here and as we have seen before, Milton makes his pagan deities his own by disposing his pantheon in a very special light. Olympus itself became for Milton a mere fiber in the fabric of displacement, one more exemplifying image of degenerated mythic truth and power: when "Jove usurping reign'd," the displaced gods on "cold Olympus rul'd the middle Air / Thir highest Heav'n" (1.514–17); the poet's muse is "Nor of the Muses nine, nor on the top / Of old Olympus . . . but Heav'nly born" (7.6–7); "wide- / Encroaching *Eve,*" some fable, "had first the rule / Of high Olympus, thence by Saturn driv'n" (10.580–83). In all this, Olympus is an image or suggestion of power gained by, and yielded to, displacement. So it is in *Windsor-Forest,* where Olympus and the goddesses are made Pope's own in much the same way, but with a very different result. When we read the passage in which our maligned couplet occurs, we must not forget that the controlling word is *not:*

> Not proud *Olympus* yields a nobler Sight,
> Tho' Gods assembled grace his tow'ring Height,
> Than what more humble Mountains offer here,
> Where, in their Blessings, all those Gods appear.
> See *Pan* with Flocks, with Fruits *Pomona* crown'd,
> Here blushing *Flora* paints th' enamel'd Ground,
> Here *Ceres'* Gifts in waving Prospect stand,
> And nodding tempt the joyful Reaper's Hand,
> Rich Industry sits smiling on the Plains,
> And Peace and Plenty tell, a STUART reigns.
>
> [ll. 33–42]

Paradoxically, Olympus is made to *yield* to our imagination what she cannot offer our sight. Olympus gives place to more humble but greater mountains,

> *Jove,* subdu'd by mortal Passion still,
> Might change *Olympus* for a nobler Hill,
>
> [ll. 233–34]

just as the vainglorious mountains of ancients and idolaters are displaced by the holy mountains of *Paradise Lost*. The Stuart monarch assimilates the dislocated mythic substance of Pan and Pomona, Flora and Ceres. Queen Anne is replete with power, they are an emptied dream.

It may be that we reach an essential point of understanding about *Windsor-Forest* when we realize that, though Anne is here presented as analagous to Eve, she also bears something of the same relation to her as she does to the pagan deities: the comparison of Anne with Eve is inevitable and even implicit in the use of the Miltonic language. But Pope's image of a controlling, reigning sovereign, who oversees toilsome industry and far-flung commerce, who must carefully manage her nation's stores so that plenty can be preserved, and who harmonizes the forces of discord into a loud chord of "Peace!" is not the image of an Eve home on her hill in Eden. The peace of *Windsor-Forest* is only (to use Clausewitz's term) *Waffenstillstand.* Windsor-Forest / England cannot be Eden, Pope tells us. To say that it can, or should be, is to distort reality and to constrict the potentialities of the future. This is a subtle but crucial part of the poem's Tory reflection on the Whiggish naïveté that obscures the massive truth embedded in *Paradise Lost.*[7]

It is the effort to return to this encased vision that is reflected by the syntax of polite rejection and declination, which in turn shapes the poet's invocation of *Paradise Lost:* "These, were my

7. For a discussion of Pope's effort "to turn the tables" on "the traditional Whiggish hatred of the Normans," see Earl R. Wasserman, *The Subtler Language: Critical Readings of Neoclassic and Romantic Poems* (Baltimore, 1959), pp. 114 ff.

Breast inspir'd with equal Flame, / Like them in Beauty, should be like in Fame" (ll. 9–10). Taken in the context of the poet's obvious abilities in the idyllic strain, the lines are in many ways comparable to Horace's paradoxical recusatio to identify himself totally with an accepted epos: magnificent epic description must somehow be joined to "si quantum cuperem possem quoque" (Ep.2.1.257). In much the same way as, in the pantheon passage, the word *not* controls and qualifies the series of mythological allusions that follow it, the poet's rhetorical hedge forces us to discriminate the non-Edenic features of a description that might otherwise seem a veritable snapshot of paradise before Satan's first visit:

> Here Hills and Vales, the Woodland and the Plain,
> Here Earth and Water seem to strive again,
> Not *Chaos*-like together crush'd and bruis'd,
> But as the World, harmoniously confus'd:
> Where Order in Variety we see,
> And where, tho' all things differ, all agree.
> Here waving Groves a checquer'd Scene display,
> And part admit and part exclude the Day;
> As some coy Nymph her Lover's warm Address
> Nor quite indulges, nor can quite repress.
>
> [ll. 11–20]

In spite of the invocation of the model of *Paradise Lost*, and in spite of the fact that Windsor Forest and Eden are both contrasted to Chaos, the poet insists on the continuity of his vision with the postlapsarian condition of the world. He cannot wish away the universal evidences of strife, confusion, dissension, sexual coyness, and sexual repression which, even if they are constrained to a *concordia discors*, are signs of an essential difference between man within and without the Eastern Gate.

The poet of *Windsor-Forest* calls upon *Paradise Lost* because it contains the English, Christian version of the massive myth he wishes to make new. It is a myth which, like the one retold in Plato's *Politicus*, not only describes a creative, ordered condition of human existence, but also intimates the successor myths of reversal and displacement and, ultimately, of reenstatement by inspired, just men—ideal preacher-*politici*. All this, Pope invokes and reenacts in his own mythic structure. A version of the Edenic age gives way to a version of Milton's age of Nimrod, a perversion of man's heroic impulses:

> Proud *Nimrod* first the bloody Chace began,
> A mighty Hunter, and his Prey was Man.
>
> [ll. 61–62]

This, in turn, is converted into peace by the talisman of poet-Granville-Anne. But, as we saw earlier, it is a distinctly sublimated state, a half-illuminated "shady Empire" where war and blood are still to be seen in "the Sylvan Chace" (ll. 371–72) and where rebellion is chained but not extinguished (cf. l. 421).

The vision of perfectibility presented in *Windsor-Forest* is, in fact, a reversal of the terms of regeneration envisioned in *Paradise Lost:* now man is encouraged to cultivate and exploit his materialistic nature rather than to alter it; the trajectory of man's expulsion from Eden becomes the route to a demi-paradise of controlled commercialism. This is Milton's vision displaced, his Paradise removed. It is this mythopoeic transportation, symbolized by the genius of England's industry and shipping, which is perhaps suggested in the "secret Transport" which "touch'd the conscious Swain": "Fair *Liberty, Britannia*'s Goddess, rears / Her chearful Head, and leads the golden Years" (ll. 90–92). This is how Pope unlocks the massive, secret spring of Christian liberty Milton had recreated. This is the poet's act of demythological recovery: "Of ancient Writ [he] unlocks the learned Store, / Consults the Dead, and lives past Ages o'er" (ll. 247–48). Britannia's goddess Liberty is also "Britannia's Standard" of liberation (l. 110):

> Oh stretch thy Reign, fair *Peace!* from Shore to Shore,
> Till Conquest cease, and Slav'ry be no more:
> Till the freed *Indians* in their native Groves
> Reap their own Fruits, and woo their Sable Loves.
>
> [ll. 407–10]

It is in the process of opening all the "Shades" of Windsor /
England (cf. l. 4), of insisting on the moral realism involved in
imagining and creating his "shady Empire" as distinct from an
unattainable Eden, that the poet has made available once more
the unaltered source of Liberty (with all its attendant promises
and dreams) enshrined in *Paradise Lost.*

In Milton's poem, we recall, the last vestige of paradise is
dislodged by the great flood:

> then shall this Mount
> Of Paradise by might of Waves be mov'd
> Out of his place, push'd by the horned flood,
> With all his verdure spoil'd, and Trees adrift
> Down the great River to the op'ning Gulf,
> And there take root an Island salt and bare.
>
> [11. 829–34]

It was in this locus of displacement that Milton, we suggested,
may have found his own prophetic hill on his own real or figur-
ative island. In *Windsor-Forest* the outflowing and displacement of demi-Eden are assigned a reversed meaning. In language remarkably similar to Milton's, postlapsarian man is
here called upon to abandon the ideal of an insular paragon
and to channel his fallen impulses into the pursuit of a sublimated postlapsarian ideal. Great River Thames, with his
"shining Horns" (l. 332), looks forward to a golden age of
transport:

> Thy Trees, fair *Windsor!* . . . shall leave their Woods,
> And half thy Forests rush into my Floods,
>   Bear *Britain*'s Thunder, and her Cross display,
> To the bright Regions of the rising Day;
> . . . .
> For me the Balm shall bleed, and Amber flow,
> The Coral redden, and the Ruby glow.
>
> [ll. 385–94]

Here we must extend our appreciation of Pope's imperial allu-
siveness by recalling that Milton sets his own trees adrift from
Eden's "Groves whose rich Trees wept odorous Gums and

Balm" (*P.L.*, 4.248). Pope's importation of "The weeping Amber or the balmy Tree" (l. 30) is itself one part of his emulation of Milton's displacement procedures. The emulation itself, a statement of displacement, gives rise to a significantly different Golden Age from that imagined by the poet of *Paradise Lost.* It is a vision of straitened, middle-state man, ambitious only of that to which postdeluvian creatures can realistically attain:

> My humble Muse, in unambitious Strains,
> Paints the green Forests and the flow'ry Plains,
> Where Peace descending bids her Olives spring,
> And scatters Blessings from her Dove-like Wing.
>
> [ll. 427–30]

In the last four lines of the poem, Pope's editors have observed, he followed the model of Virgil in returning to his own beginnings.[8] As Virgil ended the *Georgics* with the opening of the *Eclogues,* so Pope's closing couplets echo the first lines of *Spring:*

> First in these Fields I try the Sylvan Strains,
> Nor blush to sport on *Windsor's* blissful Plains:
> Fair *Thames* flow gently from thy sacred Spring,
> While on thy Banks *Sicilian* Muses sing.
>
> [ll. 1–4]

In the close of *Windsor-Forest,* we should add, the Virgilian convention is observed, even while the genius of the place is no longer Sicilian or Roman, but English:

> Ev'n I more sweetly pass my careless Days,
> Pleas'd in the silent Shade with empty Praise;
> Enough for me, that to the listning Swains
> First in these Fields I sung the Sylvan Strains.
>
> [ll. 431–34]

The poet subtly asserts his own poetic liberty, his own self-sufficiency and independence, in his own return to beginnings. His beginning fields, his poetic locus, we come to recognize,

---

8. See *TE*, 1 : 194.

are a version of Milton's removed island, of Eden displaced or redisplaced.

The "throne usurped"

But we may suspect that even in 1713 Pope's faith in the myth of English monarchical power as a cause sufficient for an Augustan utopia was far less than complete. In the very next year, in *The Rape of the Lock,* canto 3, he was exploding the dignity of Queen Anne:

> Here Thou, Great *Anna!* whom three Realms obey,
> Dost sometimes Counsel take—and sometimes *Tea.*
>
> [ll. 7–8]

Instead of the Queen's mythical power to create order with a word, we are treated to Belinda's horrific bandying of the divine Logos: *"Let Spades be Trumps!* she said, and Trumps they were"* (l. 46). As the era of the Georges lengthened out its dull tenure, Pope despaired more and more of basing the authority of his public voice on a mutual dependency of throne and poet. As Maynard Mack has said,

> The time was past when any serious writer could find his place to stand beside the throne. Dryden had managed this, and in his finest poems speaks as if the establishment, with the monarchy its center, spoke through him—the last principle of order in a disintegrating world. But for Pope, after the death of Anne, the throne as center of the dream of the civilized community has become absurd. What he gives us instead, in various versions, is intimations of a throne usurped, or a throne occupied by shadows. . . .
>
> Dryden's angle of vision was no longer available to a serious poet, but there was a possible alternative. . . . Though the throne is empty, there remains an alternative center, and a power of a different kind: the poet-king-philosopher in his grotto, midway between the garden and the river.[9]

9. *The Garden and the City,* pp. 234–36.

Pope's innovative imitation of the First Epistle of the Second Book of Horace, *To Augustus,* creates a tone of cynicism toward the king that is striking in its bitterness, especially on the score of George's neglect of the poet-king relationship and, therefore, of the heraldic office:

> Yet think great Sir! (so many Virtues shown)
> Ah think, what Poet best may make them known?
> . . . .
> How barb'rous rage subsided at your word,
> And Nations wonder'd while they dropp'd the sword!
> How, when you nodded, o'er the land and deep,
> Peace stole her wing, and wrapt the world in sleep;
> . . . .
> But Verse alas! your Majesty disdains;
> And I'm not used to Panegyric strains:
> . . . .
> 'Praise undeserv'd is scandal in disguise:'
> Well may he blush, who gives it, or receives;
> And when I flatter, let my dirty leaves
> (Like Journals, Odes, and such forgotten things
> As Eusden, Philips, Settle, writ of Kings)
> Cloath spice, line trunks, or flutt'ring in a row,
> Befringe the rails of Bedlam and Sohoe.
>
> [ll. 376–419]

Brower has remarked that the "Augustan twilight"—"the failure of the Tories, the disappointments of Pope and his friends, the death of the men who had created the brief illusion of a new literature and a new culture"—becomes, in Pope's later poetry, "a timeless image of decline and fall." [10] But we must emphasize that the authority of Pope's later voice, proclaiming, in straightforward or inverted terms, the order of a regenerate society, does not partake of that decline. Pope did not give up. His poetry is the drama of a private man in search of a public authority: George II, Pope implies, derives his kingly image from the likes of Settle; as a result, the supposed king and the

---

10. *Alexander Pope: The Poetry of Allusion* (Oxford, 1959), p. 318.

supposed poet confirm each other in their lack of true office. In
the process of demolishing the myth of George's Augustanism,
Pope makes available the convertible bricks and beams of a
new myth of poetic authority; he becomes the spokesman for a
higher secular power. This process and authority are implied
in *To Augustus*. They become explicit in the two coordinated
dialogues that make up the *Epilogue to the Satires* (1738).[11]

The central question of the *Epilogue* is raised early in the
first dialogue:

> 'Who's the Man, so near
> His Prince, that writes in Verse, and has his Ear?'
>
> [1. 45–46]

Where, in other words, is the authorized herald of England's
cultural integrity? The *Epilogue* opens with a suggestion from
the imaginary interlocutor to the poet: your poetry plagiarizes
Horace anyway; why don't you adopt his moderation, please
the crown, and thereby win the place that Horace enjoyed?

> 'Tis all from *Horace: Horace* long before ye
> Said, 'Tories call'd him Whig, and Whigs a Tory.'
>
> . . . .
>
> But *Horace*, Sir, was delicate, was nice;
> *Bubo* observes, he lash'd no sort of *Vice:*
>
> . . . .
>
> His sly, polite, insinuating stile
> Could please at Court, and make AUGUSTUS smile.
>
> [1. 7–20]

The poet rejects this suggestion, and in doing so he also rejects the Augustan solution to the problem of the poet's public authority. The established power of a corrupt Augustus
cannot distribute the heraldic office. To delude himself on
this point would be to default on his vision of the poet's highest responsibility. Sarcastically, therefore, he apologizes for
his adolescent constancy to the ideal:

11. The reader is referred to Mack, *The Garden and the City*, pp.
120 ff., for a description of the political and topical referents of the dialogues.

> Dear Sir, forgive the Prejudice of Youth:
> Adieu Distinction, Satire, Warmth, and Truth!
>
> > [1. 63–64]

If he could accept the position of George's herald, all his problems would be solved:

> Then might I sing without the least Offence,
> And all I sung should be the *Nation's Sense:*
> Or teach the melancholy Muse to mourn,
> Hang the sad Verse on CAROLINA's Urn,
> And hail her passage to the Realms of Rest,
> All Parts perform'd, and *all* her Children blest!
>
> > [1. 77–82]

But this cannot be. In the final analysis, the moral authority the king confers on the poet derives from virtue, and

> *Virtue* may chuse the high or low Degree,
> . . . .
> Dwell in a Monk, or light upon a King.
>
> > [1. 137–39]

The poet suggests that the king, in the present situation, does not have this authority. Pope does not wish to destroy the office of the herald, but he does want to change the source of its power. The king is dead; as the first dialogue ends, we find that he has given his substance to the false herald of the powers of vice:

> hers the Gospel is, and hers the Laws:
> . . . .
> Lo! at the Wheels of her Triumphal Car,
> Old *England's* Genius, rough with many a Scar.
> . . . .
> Hear her black Trumpet thro' the Land proclaim,
> That 'Not to be corrupted is the Shame.'
>
> > [1. 148–60]

In the second dialogue of the *Epilogue* the black myth is razed by the poet himself and "Old England's Genius" (which is

akin, perhaps, to what Dryden called Juvenal's "commonwealth genius") is explicitly restored.

Pope solves his problem by asserting his heraldic relation
to a legitimate power, established by virtue, which has been
displaced by the court of the degenerate Augustus. He will
be the poet of a shadow authority that is pristinely Roman
and Greek. He wil create its empire, or "court," in *his words:*

> . . . does the Court a worthy Man remove?
> That instant, I declare, he has my Love:
> I shun his Zenith, court his mild Decline;
> Thus SOMMERS once, and HALIFAX were mine.
> . . . .
> How can I PULT'NEY, CHESTERFIELD forget,
> While *Roman* Spirit charms, and *Attic* Wit:
> . . . .
> Or WYNDHAM, just to Freedom and the Throne,
> The Master of our Passions, and his own.
>
> [2. 74–89]

It is these men, and the power they represent, whom Pope
serves as anointing poet. He will not perform his offices for
anyone less. The rabble, it follows,

> may be hang'd, but not be crown'd.
> Enough for half the Greatest of these days
> To 'scape my Censure, not expect my Praise:
> Are they not rich? what more can they pretend?
> Dare they to hope a Poet for their Friend?
> What RICHELIEU wanted, LOUIS scarce could gain,
> And what young AMMON wish'd, but wish'd in vain.
>
> [2. 111–17]

Through his relationship to men like "All-accomplish'd St.
JOHN" (2. 139), he shows himself a "Friend to ev'ry worthy
mind" and can therefore speak as collective Man, who feels
"for all mankind" (2. 203–04). Nor should we doubt, the poet
proudly informs us, that proclamation thus derived has ample
power:

> Yes, I am proud; I must be proud to see
> Men not afraid of God, afraid of me:
> Safe from the Bar, the Pulpit, and the Throne,
> Yet touch'd and sham'd by *Ridicule* alone.
>
> [2. 208–11]

The poet's ridicule is the weapon that demolishes the false proclamation of the false king's false heralds:

> Ye tinsel Insects! whom a Court maintains,
> That counts your Beauties only by your Stains,
> Spin all your Cobwebs o'er the Eye of Day!
> The Muse's wing shall brush you all away:
> All his Grace preaches, all his Lordship sings,
> All that makes Saints of Queens, and Gods of Kings.
> . . . .
> Not *Waller*'s Wreath can hide the Nation's Scar,
> Nor *Boileau* turn the Feather to a Star.
>
> [2. 220–31]

Pope declares the dignity and efficacy of his public voice in terms of the full mythic glory of the prophet-herald:

> O sacred Weapon! left for Truth's defence,
> Sole Dread of Folly, Vice, and Insolence!
> To all but Heav'n-directed hands deny'd,
> The Muse may give thee, but the Gods must guide.
> Rev'rent I touch thee! but with honest zeal;
> To rowze the Watchmen of the Publick Weal.
>
> [2. 212–17]

His office does not rely on dead mythologies of kingship, though it derives "divine right" from its constituent myths. Chaining the monster results in an immense harnessing of cultural energy:

> Let Envy howl while Heav'n's whole Chorus sings,
> And bark at Honour not confer'd by Kings;
> . . . .

> Truth guards the Poet, sanctifies the line,
> And makes Immortal, Verse as mean as mine.
>
> [2. 242–47]

As we have seen in other examples of this mythopoetic mode, the herald's claim to authority is one with his kerygma. In his voice the mythic essence of English power and virtue is finally restored, though the restoration has tragic overtones. We must be careful not to mistake tragedy for despair.

The Dunciad

When "Chaos, and Eternal Night" swallow the world, there is not much left to say.[12] That, at least, is our first reaction upon reaching the conclusion of *The Dunciad*. Perhaps no other poem in English seems so cosmically despairing:

> Lo! thy dread Empire, CHAOS! is restor'd;
> Light dies before thy uncreating word.
> Thy hand, great Anarch! lets the curtain fall;
> And Universal Darkness buries All.
>
> [4. 653–56]

For a poet who had spent much of his life-breath expressing the "strong Antipathy of Good to Bad" [13] this would seem to be the gloomiest of all possible conclusions. Yet the impenetrably dark appearance of Pope's dunce-fallen world is deceptive. We must come to see that *The Dunciad* exemplifies what Maynard Mack has called "the principles of reciprocity, retribution, and rehabilitation" that in Pope's poetry generally govern nature's "relationships with men, as it heals the wounds they make in it and brings good out of the evil they do." [14] The poem's argument is characterized by an indomitable "Elasticity" (1. 186) of imagination. The poem describes uncreation and creation in ways which suggest that, though the pendulum of human existence has indeed never swung so far toward Night, or been held so long in the inertial phase—

12. Pope uses variations on the phrase at 1 : 12, 4 : 2, 13, and 630
13. *Epilogue to the Satires: dialogue* 2, 198.
14. *The Garden and the City*, p. 8.

nevertheless, even now, there is ample cause for hope. It may be that we ourselves fall into a dunce's trap when, misled by fashionable pessimism and myopic inattention, we scan *The Dunciad* for confirmation of our darkest forebodings concerning man and civilization. Misperception itself is one of the poem's grand themes.

Our discussion rightfully begins with the dissatisfactions of one of Pope's most *perceptive* critics, who finds the poem disturbing, not because it seems to offer a prophecy of chaos, but because the composition itself, in its form and content, seems lamentably chaotic. I refer to Ian Jack's complaints that *The Dunciad's* idiom is not "consistently mock-heroic" and that it suffers from "a fundamental uncertainty" about its subject, "a fatal indefiniteness of purpose." [15] The most serious implications of these criticisms were baldly stated by Joseph Warton, Jack's acknowledged instructor in viewing the poem's difficulties. Pope's stylistic "motley," Warton said, is a symptom of dangerous confusion of sacred and profane, especially in book 4, which Warton wryly likened to "introducing a crucifix into one of *Teniers'* burlesque conversation-pieces." [16]

Jack has further suggested that in his *Mac Flecknoe*-inspired poem, Pope failed because, in this instance, he chose not to emulate Dryden's "consistent following-out of the mock-heroic idea." [17] Yet we recall that in his own apocalyptic satire Dryden carefully chose *not* to follow the stylistic singleness of *Mac Flecknoe*. And the critical disapprobation he incurred from Johnson and *his* descendants is remarkably parallel to the reaction to *The Dunciad*. In fact, we might note that the poem in the Dryden canon *The Dunciad* most significantly resembles is not *Mac Flecknoe*, from which Pope borrowed the outline of duncery and its correspondences, but *The Hind and the Panther*, which offered the great theme of the satirist's

15. *Augustan Satire: Intention and Idiom in English Poetry, 1660–1750* (Oxford, 1952), pp. 128–34.

16. *An Essay on the Genius and Writings of Pope* (London, 1782), 2 : 370.

17. *Augustan Satire*, p. 134.

battle with the Antichrist who steals men's minds. The mysteries of Christianity and iniquity that are crucial to the meaning of *The Hind and the Panther* are also central to *The Dunciad.*[18] The stylistic multiplicity of both poems is also, I believe, directly related to both poets' desires to "half . . . shew" and "half veil" the "deep Intent" of "Mysteries restor'd" (4. 4–5). In both poems the diversity of styles suggests a deep disjunction in the record of reality, a disjunction that is, for the nonduncical perceiver, not a sign of chaos but an opening for profound insight.

In *The Dunciad* this disjunction is manifest not only in the dissimilar idioms of different passages but in the thematic and tonal stratification within a single passage. Recurrent quakes of wit raise to view the deepest levels of meaning and indicate an order of intelligence that is above the mere description of Dulness's evil. This striking use of disjunctive metaphor is perhaps best described as *emergent*—as being or causing an urgent issuing forth. Sir Francis Page, for example, is fitted out as one of Dulness's creatures in the following couplets:

> *Morality,* by her false Guardians drawn,
> *Chicane* in Furs, and *Casuistry* in Lawn,
> Gasps, as they straiten at each end the cord,
> And dies, when Dulness gives her Page the word.
>
>   [4. 27–30]

Sir Francis's time-serving justice suggests suborned intellect. Scriblerus innocently emphasizes Page's lackey status by imagining *"Page* here to mean no more than a *Page* or *Mute,* and to allude to the custom of strangling State Criminals in *Turkey* by Mutes or Pages" (4. 30n). But in addition to the mock-heroic bifurcation of *Page* into courtliness and savagery, there is an obvious, yet strange, third use of *Page* that throws the four lines into a totally different configuration: "her Page" is not Dulness's but Morality's (like "her false Guardians"). In

18. See Aubrey Williams, *Pope's* Dunciad: *A Study of its Meaning* (London, 1955), pp. 141 ff. For a discussion of this aspect of *The Hind and the Panther,* see my *Dryden and the Abyss of Light: A Study of* Religio Laici *and* The Hind and the Panther (New Haven, 1970), pp. 191–237.

a duncical world where corruption is so often mirrored in the
subversion of the printed word, we are not surprised to find
piratical corruption of Morality's sacred text. The composite
of Francis Page-Turkish page and Morality's printed page is
not held together by a single principle of logic. The lines
pull apart and bring to the surface a complex of absenteeism
and destructive usurpation.

A similar effect is achieved in the description of Cibber's
pyre for his much-loved, sadly bound offspring. Before the
intervention of his angel,

> The rowling smokes involve the sacrifice.
> The op'ning clouds disclose each work by turns,
> Now flames the Cid, and now Perolla burns;
> Great Caesar roars, and hisses in the fires;
> King John in silence modestly expires:
> No merit now the dear Nonjuror claims,
> Moliere's old stubble in a moment flames.
>
> [1. 248–54]

The mock-heroic affiliation of Cibber with Abraham is reen-
forced by heroic diction—*flames, wars, hisses, expires*—which,
upon closer examination, collapses into effete pyrotechny,
roaring laughter, angry hissing, and theatrical flop. Yet, as in
the previous passage, the mock-heroic dislocation gives way to
a third level of meaning. We come to understand that Cibber
averts his eyes (4. 247) from beholding his own exposure.

Merciless payment is exacted from the goddess's son for his
many thefts. The world is to be shown

> How here [Cibber] sipp'd, how there he plunder'd snug
> And suck'd all o'er, like an industrious Bug.
> Here lay poor Fletcher's half-eat scenes, and here
> The Frippery of crucify'd Moliere;
> There hapless Shakespear, yet of Tibbald sore,
> Wish'd he had blotted for himself before.
>
> [1. 129–34]

When the flames of the sacrifice "disclose," by "turns," the
parts of his works, we find that Cibber's *Ximena* is principally
Corneille's *Le Cid,* his *Caesar in Aegypt* is Fletcher and Mas-

singer's *The False One,* his *Papal Tyranny in the Reign of King John* is Shakespeare's *King John,* and his *Non-Juror* is Molière's *Tartuffe.* The main purpose of this reckoning is not, in any sense, poetic justice. Rather, it is to suggest that Dulness's uncreating power is a dangerous parasitism or displacement of other men's imaginative creations. Dulness must begin with Shakespeare's or Morality's page. Her activity is in transmutation—of gold to "lead"—in the wrong "turn" of the materials of art that others have repeatedly readapted *in the service* of culture. Dulness has no imagination. Her patchwork is deadly vampirism:

> A past, vamp'd,[19] future, old, reviv'd, new piece,
> 'Twixt Plautus, Fletcher, Shakespear, and Corneille,
> Can make a Cibber, Tibbald, or Ozell.
>
> > [1. 284–86]

We must not underestimate Pope's emphasis on Dulness's *activity.* She is the daughter of Chaos, a "Force inertly strong" (4. 7), but she herself is described in the poem as being markedly energetic. The "Bentley" of Pope's footnote world reminds us that Dulness is "not inert." She

> includes (as we see by the Poet's own words) Labour, Industry, and some degree of Activity and Boldness: a ruling principle not inert, but turning topsy-turvy the Understanding, and inducing an Anarchy or confused State of Mind. This remark ought to be carried along with the reader throughout the work; and without this caution he will be apt to mistake the Importance of many of the Characters, as well as of the Design of the Poet. Hence it is that some have complained he chuses too mean a subject, and imagined he employs himself, like Domitian, in killing flies; whereas those who have the true key will find

19. It is quite possible that Pope intended a pun in *vamp'd.* The primary meaning of the word is clearly *patch'd.* But the *OED* informs us that the word *vampire* was taking its place in England during the 1730s and 1740s. Given *The Dunciad's* concern with witchcraft (see below), it is not hard to believe that Pope's use of the word—which appears also in the 1728 edition—furnishes a new *de quo* for the lexicographers.

he sports with nobler quarry, and embraces a larger compass. [1. 15 n]

The pedant has furnished a valuable insight but, with characteristic heavy-handedness, his learned allusion makes him fall
short of the mark. Pope's subject *is* flies and they are also the
vehicle engaged for reaching his larger compass. Dulness is
Lord of the Flies, Beelzebub in another guise. In fact, the
"Chaos dark and deep" that is the main subject of *The Dunciad* is described, early and late in the poem, as Dulness's in-
sectarium,

> Where nameless Somethings in their causes sleep,
> 'Till genial Jacob, or a warm Third day,
> Call forth each mass, a Poem, or a Play:
> How hints, like spawn, scarce quick in embryo lie,
> How new-born nonsense first is taught to cry,
> Maggots half-form'd in rhyme exactly meet,
> And learn to crawl upon poetic feet.
>
> [1. 56–62]

Dulness's progeny are

> As thick as bees o'er vernal blossoms . . .
> As thick as eggs at Ward in Pillory;
>
> [3. 33–34]

> . . . thick as Locusts black'ning all the ground.
>
> [4. 397]

Their motivation is "insect lust" (4. 415). The larger compass
of Dulness's insectlike nature is mirrored in the structure of
her darkened solar system:

> None want a place, for all their Centre found,
> Hung to the Goddess, and coher'd around.
> Not closer, orb in orb, conglob'd are seen
> The buzzing Bees about their dusky Queen.
>   The gath'ring number, as it moves along,
> Involves a vast involuntary throng,
> Who gently drawn, and struggling less and less,

> Roll in her Vortex, and her pow'r confess.
> Not those alone who passive own her laws,
> But who, weak rebels, more advance her cause.
>
> [4. 77–86]

Dulness's vorticose orbit, itself drifting blindly, curbs and eliminates progressive motion. Each particle of her citizenry is, in fact,

> set on Metaphysic ground to prance,
> Show all his paces, not a step advance.
>
> [4. 265–66]

In reality Dulness recognizes no *"Nous"*—no "first cause" (4. 244 and n.); and she has "No cause"—no *cause finale*—of her own (cf. 4. 340). For Dulness all cause reduces to the material and formal. Her votaries, who are said to "sleep" in their own larval "causes," sound the death knell of mythic *telos*. With absurd insect temerity her vaunt-courier proclaims:

> Let others creep by timid steps, and slow,
> On plain Experience lay foundations low,
> By common sense to common knowledge bred,
> And last, to Nature's Cause thro' Nature led.
> All-seeing in thy mists, we want no guide,
> Mother of Arrogance, and Source of Pride!
> We nobly take the high Priori Road,
> And reason downward, till we doubt of God:
> Make Nature still incroach upon his plan;
> And shove him off as far as e'er we can:
> Thrust some Mechanic Cause into his place;
> Or bind in Matter, or diffuse in Space.
> Or, at one bound o'er-leaping all his laws,
> Make God Man's Image, Man the final Cause.
>
> [4. 465–78]

Dulness's imago, bred by the high priori method of solipsism and intuitionism, is at best an infantile copy of the infantile parent. Here there is no room for meaningful growth. There is a deadening circularity in the assumptions that "Man's whole frame is obvious to a *Flea*" (4. 238) and that men had "Reason giv'n them but to study *Flies*" (4. 454).

Order of intelligence is gone; and so is motive independence. The lepidopterist has become the insect; the butterfly's *starting* is the man's *beginning* and his end. In a telling parallel to Eve's postnatal narcissism, he testifies:

> I saw, and started from its vernal bow'r
> The rising game, and chac'd from flow'r to flow'r.
> It fled, I follow'd; now in hope, now pain;
> It stopt, I stopt; it mov'd, I mov'd again.
>
> [4. 425–28]

Mankind itself has been *hatched*: "Lo! one vast Egg produces human race" (3. 248).

Dryden and Swift had both worked brilliant variations on the metaphor of insect activity as cultural degeneration. But it remained for Pope to identify it with a principle of uncreative causation and to build around it a vision of *regeneration*. Pope's "industrious Bug," which "suck'd all o'er" (1. 130), is associated with the Mechanic Cause that is seen to incroach upon God's final Cause. The insect-man and the machine are seen together early in book 3, in the passage which, as he told Spence, Pope had spun off from the *disjecta materia* of his own intellectual adolescence.[20] The lines offer an emblem of cultural infantilism:

> As man's Maeanders to the vital spring
> Roll all their tides, then back their circles bring;
> Or whirligigs, twirl'd round by skilful swain,
> Suck the thread in, then yield it out again:
> All nonsense thus, of old or modern date,
> Shall in thee centre, from thee circulate.
>
> [3. 55–60]

This is Dulness's myth. This, as Dryden put it, is her vision of tautology. But Dulness's "Mechanic Cause" is shown to be

20. See Joseph Spence, *Observations, Anecdotes, and Characters of Books and Men Collected from Conversation,* ed. James M. Osborn (Oxford, 1966), 1 : 16–19.

much less than perpetual. She and her sons cannot "yield" and "suck" endlessly. The whirligig breaks down:

> the Muses, on their racks,
> Scream like the winding of ten thousand jacks:
> Some free from rhyme or reason, rule or check,
> Break Priscian's head, and Pegasus's neck;
> Down, down they larum, with impetuous whirl,
> The Pindars, and the Miltons of a Curl.
>
> [3. 159–64]

This shattering of Curll's "Miltons"—the parasitized Miltonic imitations (such as Philips's *Cider*) which Curll printed and reprinted—must somehow release a genuine Miltonic essence.

The Dunciad describes Dulness's attempt to insure the "cause" of her "continuance" (it is her only cause), yet there is more than a little prophecy in the early description of Cibber "pensive among his Books, giving up the Cause, and apprehending the Period of [Dulness's] Empire." [21] When we hear his anguished apostrophe,

> Dulness! whose good old cause I yet defend,
> With whom my Muse began, with whom shall end,
>
> [1. 165–66]

we must remind ourselves again that there can be no equation between "Dulness" and "Chaos and eternal Night" (1. 12). Though Dulness was "born a Goddess" and "never dies" (1. 18), her empire is no more than co-temporary with mankind and with the succession of dunces who supply her state: she has "rul'd, in native Anarchy, the mind"—*of man* (1. 16). Dulness thrasonically misinterprets the apocalyptic prophecy supplied by the "sable Sorc'rer" of book 3:

> ten-horn'd fiends and Giants rush to war.
> Hell rises, Heav'n descends, and dance on Earth:
> Gods, imps, and monsters, music, rage, and mirth,
> A fire, a jigg, a battle, and a ball,
> 'Till one wide conflagration swallows all.

21. *TE*, 5 : 266.

> Thence a new world to Nature's laws unknown,
> Breaks out refulgent, with a heav'n its own.
>
> [3. 236–42]

Her "Angel," "Immortal Rich," controls "these worlds" (3. 255–61), but she is too quick to claim the "new world," a world unlike "native Anarchy," for her own.

At the beginning of book 4 Dulness sets out to fulfill her destiny:

> Then rose the Seed of Chaos, and of Night,
> To blot out Order, and extinguish Light,
> Of dull and venal a new World to mold,
> And bring Saturnian days of Lead and Gold.
>
> [4. 13–16]

We wonder why a "new World" of "dull and venal" will not be merely redundant. Dulness, indeed, is planning her own eternal tautology, one which would cancel even eschatological succession. But this was not meant to be. As the poem draws to a close, Dull and Venal are themselves abrogated in the general doom. Before the poet and his muse (whose end was long since prophesied) dissolve into asterisk silence, we see that not only Right but Wrong also must perish in order for the true new world to begin:

> O Muse! relate (for you can tell alone,
> Wits have short Memories, and Dunces none)
> Relate, who first, who last resign'd to rest;
> Whose Heads she partly, whose completely blest;
> What Charms could Faction, what Ambition lull,
> The Venal quiet, and intrance the Dull;
> 'Till drown'd was Sense, and Shame, and Right, and
>   Wrong—
> O sing, and hush the Nations with thy Song!
>
> [4. 619–26]

Dulness's "Muse obeys the Pow'r" (4. 628), the power of "Mysteries restor'd" (4. 5). The "sable Throne" which is ushered in is not Dulness's but, as Pope emphasizes, "Of Night Primæval, and of Chaos old" (4. 629–30); it belongs to the

parents, not the "Seed." [22] The "dull of ancient days" (1. 294)
and "the Antichrist of wit" (2. 16) have had their season.
Man's dominion and Dulness's empire have together reached
their "Period."

At this point we must remind ourselves that Chaos and
Eternal Night, like much else in the machinery of *The
Dunciad,* are endowed with an identity specifically dependent
upon our acquaintance with *Paradise Lost.* Indeed, as Aubrey
Williams has remarked, Pope's imitations of Milton's poem
form one dimension of *The Dunciad*'s meaning: "the Miltonic
resources enable the poet to . . . shadow forth, in metaphor,
the implicit evil in duncery, and to associate the dulness of
his poem with the diabolism of *Paradise Lost.*" Williams
makes clear that Pope is able to reveal the true "Intent" (4. 4)
of Dulness and her dunces by constant use of the imagery of
chaos, "most especially . . . the imagery of Milton's Chaos.
. . . For what the *Dunciad* is 'about' is in one sense the ful-
filment of Satan's vow to restore to Chaos all creation." [23] In
Paradise Lost, we recall, all Satan's malicious vows serve "but
to bring forth / Infinite goodness" (1. 217–18). His "dark
intent" (9. 162) is merely an awesome stimulus to God's transforming causality: "Good out of evil to create" (7. 188) and
"evil turn to good" (12. 471). Even in the darkest moments of
his poem Milton carefully preserved the faith that after night
must come day, that, in fact, holy light can only be reached by
passing through, by descending to, darkness: [24]

> I sung of *Chaos* and *Eternal Night,*
> Taught by the heav'nly Muse to venture down
> The dark descent, and up to reascend,

22. Pope and Warburton emphasize (4 : 2 n.) that "the Restoration of
their Empire"—Night's and Chaos's—"is the action of the poem." Mack,
The Garden and the City, p. 152, discusses the contemporary allusive implications of these and related phrases.

23. *Pope's* Dunciad, pp. 131–39.

24. See Don Cameron Allen, "Milton and the Descent to Light," reprinted in *Milton: Modern Essays in Criticism,* ed. Arthur E. Barker
(New York, 1965), pp. 177–95.

Though hard and rare: thee [holy Light] I revisit safe,
And feel thy sovran vital Lamp; but thou
Revisit'st not these eyes, that roll in vain
To find thy piercing ray, and find no dawn;
So thick a drop serene hath quencht thir Orbs,
Or dim suffusion veil'd. . . .

. . . .
. . . not to me returns
Day, or the sweet approach of Ev'n or Morn,
Or sight of vernal bloom, or Summer's Rose,
Or flocks, or herds, or human face divine;
But cloud instead, and ever-during dark
Surrounds me.

[3. 18–46]

When Pope sat down to write the "Greater Dunciad," to
stake out its limits and to formulate its functioning, it is clear
that he thought, and wished us to think, of Milton. The opening lines, as Williams has noticed, are a veritable "Miltonic
medley": [25]

> Yet, yet a moment, one dim Ray of Light,
> Indulge, dread Chaos, and eternal Night!
> Of darkness visible so much be lent,
> As half to shew, half veil the deep Intent.
> Ye Pow'rs! whose Mysteries restor'd I sing,
> To whom Time bears me on his rapid wing,
> Suspend a while your Force inertly strong,
> Then take at once the Poet and the Song.

Phrases from Milton's "How Soon Hath Time" are combined
with a barrage of ammunition from widely separated parts of
Paradise Lost (e.g. "darkness visible," 1. 63, and "dark intent,"
9. 162), to make Milton's allusive presence deeply felt. Particularly important in these lines, and in the lines that mark
the uttermost bound of the fourth book and of *The Dunciad*
as a whole, is the passage quoted above from Milton's invocation to Light. The Miltonic parallel suggests that the poet of

25. *Pope's* Dunciad, p. 137.

The Dunciad is in his own night phase, his own purposeful yet painful descent. Like Milton, too, he sings of Chaos and Eternal Night and begs the intercession of one ray of light to pierce a "dim suffusion veil'd," to illumine a "human face divine." In the close of *The Dunciad,* "Religion blushing veils her sacred fires" (4. 649), "Nor human Spark is left, nor Glimpse divine" (4. 652). Milton remains surrounded by "ever-during dark"; and Pope is buried in "Universal Darkness" (4. 656). The great difference between the passages, of course, is that Milton seeks light from the power of "Celestial Light" (3. 51), while Pope supplicates the indulgence of the powers of darkness. But the difference is more apparent and ironic than real. Pope does not ask Chaos and Night to furnish the ray itself, but only to "indulge" its passage. The light itself is generated by a far other source, much the same mysterious source, in fact, that is destined to convert Satanic darkness to holy light in *Paradise Lost*. In the modern world (perhaps in post-Restoration England particularly), Michael prophesies, the forces of Satan will relentlessly attempt to pervert good to evil ends:

> Wolves shall succeed for teachers, grievous Wolves,
> Who all the sacred mysteries of Heav'n
> To thir own vile advantages shall turn.

[12. 508-10]

But God's mysterious power transmutes Satan's evil and returns it to good:

> so shall the World go on,
> To good malignant, to bad men benign,
> Under her own weight groaning, till the day
> Appear of respiration to the just,
> And vengeance to the wicked, at return
> Of him so lately promis'd to thy aid,
> The Woman's seed, obscurely . . . foretold,
>
> . . . .
> . . . to dissolve
> *Satan* with his perverted World.

[12. 537-47]

We saw earlier that the myth of the seed, "obscurely" told, ultimately emerges as a pervasive mystery in *Paradise Lost*. It must be related in "mysterious terms" (10. 173) because it concerns the sacred mystery of the Incarnation, which can only be gradually comprehended by human understanding. Milton conceives of the visible signs of the Incarnation in historical, apocalyptic terms: Christ came, and will come again, to perfect the world. Pope, clearly, decided to follow the outlines of his Miltonic model when he chose to conclude his poem with a song of "Mysteries restor'd" (4. 5). Even slashing Bentley can see the original Miltonic mold, though, with his characteristic pedantry, he detours us to the wrong poem: "the Author in this work had indeed a *deep Intent;* there were in it *Mysteries* . . . which he durst not fully reveal, and doubtless in divers verses (according to Milton)—*more is meant than meets the ear."* [26]

But for Pope, in 1742, Milton's prophetic, historical formulation of God's greater mysteries may have come to seem somewhat cloudy and even irrelevant. As a young man, Pope himself, in the *Messiah,* had been satisfied to look beyond the welter of this life and this time, to a distant point where "The Light Himself shall shine / Reveal'd; and God's eternal Day be thine" (ll. 103–04). But his development as a poet had created in him the conviction that verse must represent the union of the local and the universal.

It may not be too much to say that Milton's millenialism seemed as alien to Pope as his pastoralism did to Dryden. There is, of course, no reason to suspect that Pope had lost faith in Christian eschatology. But in most systems of belief, Christianity not excepted, there is usually a wide latitude in the precise designation of the time and place of eschatological events. The stage-play apocalypse with which *The Dunciad* concludes—"Thy hand, great Anarch! lets the curtain fall"— is perhaps, among other things, an ironic reflection on Milton's apocalypse, even while it affirms certain leading features of Milton's prophetic mode. In fact, *The Dunciad* as a whole represents an ironic rendering of the mysteries that are climac-

26. *Il Penseroso,* l. 120.

tic in *Paradise Lost*—the "sacred mysteries" turned to and
from "vile advantages"—the mysteries of Incarnation and of
iniquity. These were the restored mysteries, the rites in which
an emblem-making poet and a Roman Catholic could participate by creating a poem of ironic dualities. The product, in
many respects, is distinctly one of local manufacture. This
must be demonstrated in some detail.[27]

Pope's fascination with the idea of a mock Mass was long-
standing. In a famous passage of *The Rape of the Lock,* we
recall, Belinda officiates in a hazy, transubstantiating rite that
is not blasphemous only because it is totally devoid of mind,
malicious or otherwise:

> rob'd in White, the Nymph intent adores
> With Head uncover'd, the *Cosmetic* Pow'rs.
> A heav'nly Image in the Glass appears,
> To that she bends, to that her Eyes she rears;
> Th'inferior Priestess, at her Altar's side,
> Trembling, begins the sacred Rites of Pride.
> . . . .
> The various Off'rings of the World appear;
> . . . .
> The Tortoise here and Elephant unite,
> Transform'd to *Combs.*[28]
>
> [1. 123–36]

We have already seen that in *The Dunciad* Dulness's "magic
gift" (2. 137) is her transubstantiating ingestion. In book 4,
as the universe moves closer and closer to radical transforma-
tion, the metaphor of an anti-Eucharist becomes unmistakable: [29]

27. Though my discussion focuses on the theological significance of
The Dunciad's satiric rites, they also possess a vast political dimension,
which has been described by Mack, *The Garden and the City,* pp. 150 ff.

28. Pope had another proving ground for distortions of the Roman
Mass in *Eloisa to Abelard.*

29. Cf. Maynard Mack, " 'Wit and Poetry and Pope': Some Observations
on his Imagery," in *Eighteenth-Century English Literature: Modern Essays in Criticism,* ed. James L. Clifford (New York, 1959), pp. 29–30.

On some, a Priest succinct in amice white
Attends; all flesh is nothing in his sight!
Beeves, at his touch, at once to jelly turn,
And the huge Boar is shrunk into an Urn:
The board with specious miracles he loads,
Turns Hares to Larks, and Pigeons into Toads.
Another (for in all what one can shine?)
Explains the *Seve* and *Verdeur* of the Vine.
What cannot copious Sacrifice attone?
Thy Treufles, Perigord! thy Hams, Bayonne!
With French Libation, and Italian Strain,
Wash Bladen white, and expiate Hays's stain.
Knight lifts the head, for what are crowds undone
To three essential Partridges in one?

[4. 549–62]

Pope, of course, did not invent the mock Mass. The anti-rite had a long and infamous history.[30] Its origins and continuance were variously affiliated with a spectrum of pagan and Manichaean dualisms which orthodox Christianity desperately battled to erase, never with complete success (not even in our own time, twentieth-century enlightenment notwithstanding). Before the seventeenth century, the antirite seems sometimes to have had strong connections with muted protests of the oppressed against corrupt clericalism: Satan was worshiped as the head of the visible church, the real "synagogue of Satan" described by John, while God was the head of an invisible church that had little power on earth. The rite and its intention were, to say the least, despairingly confused. But by the seventeenth century, and in France particularly, the more purely criminal and maniacal aspects of the antirite seem to have dominated.

Perhaps because of the secrecy and anonymity of the observance, or perhaps because of the fecund imaginations of would-be witnesses (many of them under torture), there were reportedly no limits to the sacrilege, obscenity, and mere gross-

30. See H. T. F. Rhodes, *The Satanic Mass: A Criminological Study* (London, 1968).

ness practiced by the celebrants of the mock Mass (frequently
called the Black Mass in modern times). Under the direction
of the chief officiant, the so-called Ancient One (female), and
her first lieutenant (male), the Asperges could be turned to
urination, the Offertory to child-murder or defilement of the
host in sterile sexual acts. The gruesome details are endless
and nebulous. In the reign of the Sun King, abuses of this
kind reached their peak and seem to have attracted many of
the nobility, among them one of the royal mistresses, the
Marchioness of Montespan. England seems to have escaped
the most extreme manifestations of the Black Mass, but Englishmen were not ignorant of goings-on across the channel; nor
were they totally free of all forms of the antirite. In fact, one
of Pope's dunces, Thomas Heywood (cf. 1. 98), a minor authority on witchcraft and Satanism, explained to his seventeenth-century contemporaries how the devil worshiper "is
commanded to renounce his Faith and Baptisme, the Eucha-
rist, and other holy things." Heywood's account contains less
information than innuendo, but that was itself the ambience
of the "contrary" mystery celebrations: "as the Divell is
alwayes," says Heywood, "adverse to his Creator, so hee will
be worshipped with contrarie Rites and ceremonies." [31]

We should note, however, that the history of the Black
Mass in England is chiefly remarkable for turning the antirite to burlesque—a burlesque, however, with its own dualistic,
blasphemous, obscene, and gross intentions. The English burlesque "contrarie Rites" were not to come into public glory
until around 1753, when Paul Whitehead organized the Med-
menhamite Mass near Twickenham. But burlesquing of this
kind had reached such proportions in the first decades of the
century that an alarmed royal edict was issued against it already in 1721. The central figures in this activity were noble
members of such clubs as the Hell-Fires. Philip, Duke of
Wharton (1698–1731), served as president of one of these

---

31. Thomas Heywood, *The Hierarchie of the Blessed Angels* (London,
1635), pp. 472–73. As an editor of Shakespeare, Pope may have known that
the book contained an early reference to "Mellifluous . . . Will" (p. 206).

clubs. His wit is, in fact, alluded to by Pope in the *Epistle* . . . *to . . . Cobham:*

> Tho' wond'ring Senates hung on all he spoke,
> The Club must hail him master of the joke.
>
> [ll. 184–85]

In his dramatic conversion to piety, Wharton repented of more than flippant humor. A contemporary censor tells us that the Hell-Fires aimed at "transcendant malignity, deriding the forms of religion as a trifle . . . ; by a natural progression from the form they turn to the substance; with Lucifer they fly at Divinity. The third person of the Trinity is what they peculiarly attack; by the following specimen you may judge of their good will: *i.e.,* their calling for a Holy-Ghost-pye at the tavern." [32]

It is probably no accident that the mysterious fourth book of *The Dunciad* relates, in various ways, to many of the chief figures in the English inverted Mass. The so-called Sub-Prior at Medmenham Abbey, for example, was to be John Montagu, fourth earl of Sandwich. In and out of (and likely, before) the abbey, Sandwich was known as a grinning Satanist. A contemporary print, attributed to Hogarth, shows a mock-celebrant in whose halo we see Sandwich's broad smile as he views the Black Mass scene of crude altar, naked *bona dea,* spilled chalice, open missal, and half-eaten "Holy-Ghost-pye." [33] If Sutherland is correct in nominating Montagu the "likeliest candidate" for the Mummius of book 4,[34] it seems possible that Pope was thinking of Mummius's membership in associations besides the Royal Society and the Egyptian Club. Paul Whitehead, the Medmenham organizer himself, figures in the writing of the fourth book of *The Dunciad* in at least two ways: Dulness's great Yawn (4. 606–15) was probably influenced by Whitehead's *The State Dunces;* and the lines con-

32. Quoted by E. Beresford Chancellor, *The Lives of the Rakes* (London, 1924), 3 : 4.

33. See Rhodes, *The Satanic Mass,* p. 149.

34. *TE,* 5 : 449–50.

cerning the "deep Free-Masons" who "join the silent race" (4. 571) allude, at least in part, to the mock-Masonic procession organized by Whitehead on 9 March 1741.[35] Pope, like Whitehead and like the Gregorians and Gormogons (cf. 4. 576), obviously delighted in ridicule of Freemasonry but, like them too, we must add, he relished the ritual of the ridicule.

The mock Mass of *The Dunciad* is far more extensive than the "specious miracles" of the "Priest succinct in amice white" (4. 549 ff.). In gross outline, a good deal of the action of the poem offers, in appropriately mangled sequence, a blasphemous contrary mass in which the ultimate dream of Satanic displacement seems to take place:[36] the body and soul of God's universe are assaulted in an attempt to turn intelligence to confusion, good to evil, light to darkness. In one sense the action of *The Dunciad* consists of a protracted fulfillment of the aborted "sacrifice" of Cibber's works that is the first action of the narrative. It is preceded by a mock confiteor,

"O born in sin, and forth in folly brought!
Works damn'd, or to be damn'd! (your father's fault) . . . ,"
                                                    [1. 225–26]

and ushered in by what may be a version of the incensing of the altar,

And thrice he lifted high the Birth-day brand,
And thrice he dropt it from his quiv'ring hand;
Then lights the structure, with averted eyes:
The rowling smokes involve the sacrifice.
                                                    [1. 245–48]

For burlesquing of this kind, the "contrarie Rites and ceremonies" of the Black Mass tradition had suggested ample precedent, as they had also for what might be intended, in

35. See Sutherland's note on these lines and *TE*, 5 : 473 for his comment on Pope's somewhat problematical relationship to the Freemasons. Mack, *The Garden and the City*, p. 189, discusses aspects of Whitehead's relation to Pope.

36. Distortion of the order of the Roman Mass was itself a prominent feature of the Satanic Mass.

part, as a preparatory asperges of urination (in book 2) or for
the obscene defilement of the sacred mass and the sanctum
sanctorum in book 3:

> in her Temple's last recess inclos'd,
> On Dulness' lap th' Anointed head repos'd.
> Him close she curtains round with Vapours blue,
> And soft besprinkles with Cimmerian dew.
> Then raptures high the seat of Sense o'erflow,
> Which only heads refin'd from Reason know.
>
> [ll. 1–6]

There are terrifying ambiguities in "her Temple's last recess,"
"Cimmerian dew," and "raptures high." One suspects that
"the seat of Sense," which must overflow, is very much like
the "Protuberancy," described by Swift, that causes a "certain
Great Prince" to go to war.[37] The effect of sublimation is the
same:

> Hence the Fool's Paradise, the Statesman's Scheme,
> The air-built Castle, and the golden Dream,
> The Maid's romantic wish, the Chemist's flame,
> And Poet's vision of eternal Fame.
>
> [3. 9–12]

One could speculate endlessly on parallels that Dulness's rite
creates to elements in the Roman Mass. Suffice it to say that
her transforming miracle concludes with a parody of the *Ite,
missa est,* "Go, this is the dismissal": [38]

> Then blessing all, "Go Children of my care!
> To Practice now from Theory repair.
> All my Commands are easy, short, and full:
> My Sons! be proud, be selfish, and be dull. . . ."
>
> [4. 579–82]

37. *A Tale of a Tub,* ed. A. C. Guthkelch and D. Nichol Smith (Oxford, 1958), pp. 163–64.

38. François Amiot, *History of the Mass,* trans. Lancelot C. Shepppard (New York, 1959), p. 132, points out that the phrase has sometimes been misunderstood to mean "Go, now your mission is beginning."

The poem ends with a burlesque of the prologue of the Gospel of St. John, the *In principio erat verbum* that concludes the Roman Mass: "Light dies before thy uncreating word" (4. 654).

The Black Mass of *The Dunciad* represents the lower depths of the poet's downward flight into chaos. It constitutes a frightening immersion in the imagination of evil, which, like Milton's descent, is meant to expose evil and, thereby, to reach light. As in Milton's poem, too, evil accomplishes its partial goals but they ultimately serve the ends of goodness: Cibber's protracted sacrifice, Dulness's "specious" miracle, is ultimately fulfilled; but it turns out to be one part of the overall immolation of the dunces that is the business of the poem. *The Dunciad* is that rare and solemn thing (which some mistakenly regard as uniquely modern), a deadly serious burlesque. What gives this burlesque its special power and import is the fact that its target is itself a potentially fatal burlesque of sacred Christian rite. In lines added to book 1 in the revised four-book version of *The Dunciad,* Cibber is made to prophesy, just as he begins his burnt-offering, that his writings heaped on the altar are

> Soon to that mass of Nonsense to return,
> Where things destroy'd are swept to things unborn.
>
> [1. 241–42]

The duncical "mass of Nonsense" has two meanings, of which the less evident is the more significant: the enterprise of Dulness is to pervert the mystery of God's incarnated goodness into a mystery of transubstantiating iniquity. The desperate mission of *The Dunciad*'s controlling irony is precarious and even dangerous in the highest degree: it is to present a transubstantiating burlesque of a falsely transubstantiating burlesque; it is to offer up a sacrificial mass on the body of a perverted mass which is in the process of sacrificing all goodness and intelligence. The achievement of the poem consists of ritual ridicule, of mysterious satirizing of satiric mysteries.

It was Pope's way of restoring the mysteries described in *Paradise Lost*. Man's heel is undoubtedly bruised in the process, but Satan's head is well-nigh crushed.

Dulness and her sons serve as unwitting agents of a higher cause. Her insect cloud blindly "moves along" (4. 81), as if to a foreordained place and time. Even Dulness's best-laid anarchy leads to one great end. Under the guidance of the poet's irony, there emerges an ineluctable causality between her subversiveness and God's fulfillment. Her mysteries and those of Christianity are, in fact, continuous. What might be regarded as Pope's rather programmatic handling of the contrary mass may suggest that he was consciously following out preformulated Enlightenment ideas concerning the relation of Christian mysteries to pagan ones.[39] At this distance it is unlikely that we will ever pinpoint these ideas, but perhaps we can catch a glimpse of the kind of thinking that, in addition to Milton's model, helped determine Pope's procedures.

Beginning in 1726, at latest, Viscount Bolingbroke confided to Pope his philosophical views in extended conversations and letters, of which the *Essays* and *Minutes* published in 1753 (and addressed to Pope) are in some sense a record (perhaps a very imperfect one).[40] Among a myriad of other opinions and observations, Bolingbroke supports the view that Christian mysteries did, in some ways, evolve from pagan ritual. This, he feels, should not shock us because "the theology of the heathen was founded on original truth." [41] Bolingbroke finds comfort rather than vexation in the probable continuity of human worship. A core of religious truth, he argues, is somehow always preserved—in spite of the intentions of perverting priests—though it is often forced to assume an inappropriate form:

39. An interesting—but, I think, mistaken—attempt to understand this relation is William J. Howard's "The Mystery of the Cibberian 'Dunciad,' " *Studies in English Literature* 8 (1968) : 463–74.

40. I am indebted to Sutherland's suggestion (*TE*, 5 : xxi n.) that "the metaphysical part of *The Dunciad* . . . probably owed a good deal . . . to Bolingbroke."

41. *The Works of . . . Lord Viscount Bolingbroke* (London, 1809), 6 : 52.

genuine theism [has] been at different times, and in different places, discovered, established, corrupted, lost, and renewed. [In some places] Christianity has been established on the ruins of polytheism and idolatry, and has been rooted up again in its turn.[42]

Bolingbroke believed that Christian mysteries were a necessary concession to the "unnatural and profane mixtures of human imagination." [43] He regarded the Church's mysteries as a kind of palliative to primitive religious impulses and, what is perhaps most important for our discussion, as a vehicle for salvaging and converting the essential mythic tenor:

the foolish creeds and the burlesque rites of paganism were rendered, in the preparatory mysteries, a little less shocking to the common sense of those in whom knowledge began to get the better of prejudice. But this reformation and improvement could not be carried far at once. Allegory served to disguise ignorance, and to muffle up even knowledge in mystery among the vulgar. To cure this abuse, to take off these masks, and to lay allegory aside whenever it did not serve to illustrate truth, and to improve or facilitate knowledge, required time: and men, who had been bred in darkness, were to be accustomed to the light by degrees. . . . There are good, and, I think, sufficient, grounds to be persuaded, that the whole system of polytheism was unravelled in the greater mysteries, or that no more of it was retained, than what might be rendered consistent with monotheism, with the belief of one Supreme Self-existent Being.[44]

How this unraveling was accomplished, or how true religion was *restored,* was beyond Bolingbroke. He had a general distaste for anything irrational, and he urged Pope not to waver in what had apparently been his concurrent aversion. In another place, he reminded Pope

42. Ibid., pp. 243–60.
43. Ibid., 5 : 92.
44. Ibid., 6 : 35–36.

of a passage you quoted to me once, with great applause, from a sermon of Foster, and to this effect: "Where mystery begins, religion ends." . . . If you have changed your mind, think again, and examine further.[45]

The evidence of *The Dunciad* suggests that Pope had become convinced that, as a Christian poet, he could not afford a cool disdain for mystery. Rather, his way was to seek a poetic unraveling of Dulness's antichristian mysteries. Bolingbroke had noted that

> the inhabitants of the Theban dynasty . . . held, that there was no God but one, and this one God was represented under a human figure by some, with an egg, the symbol of the world, coming out of his mouth.[46]

Pope may be using this kind of primitive recognition to further his own poetic aims. Even a dunce, in a lucid moment induced by "a ray of Reason," can say, "Learn, ye Dunces! not to scorn your God" (3. 224–25). Dulness's distorted picture of the universe, in which God is created in the image of a spawning man, contains a convertible perception: "Lo! one vast Egg produces human race" (3. 248). Mankind, at least, is seen as having been created by an ordaining power, a power whose influence may yet be restored when the excrescences of idolatrous misapprehension have been cleared away.

In *The Dunciad,* as in *An Essay on Man,* "All subsists by elemental strife" and all things lead to "the Universal Cause." [47] The function of the poet remains what it was in former times when the

> Follow'r of God or friend of human-kind,
> Poet or Patriot, rose but to restore

45. Ibid., 5 : 112.

46. Ibid., 6 : 51–52.

47. *An Essay on Man,* 1 : 169 and 4 : 35. For an interesting discussion of these ideas, see F. E. L. Priestly, "Pope and the Great Chain of Being," in *Essays in English Literature,* ed. Millar MacLure (Toronto, 1964), pp. 213–28.

The Faith and Moral, Nature gave before;
Re-lum'd her ancient light, not kindled new;
If not God's image, yet his shadow drew.[48]

The Dunciad is a poem of significant shadows in a seemingly
blind alley of civilization.[49] Our attention is spasmodically
riveted by ghosts of departed ideals that flit through the four
books. Yet there is a larger, more horrific shadow whose
presence we feel powerfully but whose outline we barely per-
ceive. The "gloomy Clerk" (4. 459) makes us aware of divine
nearness when he cries out to Dulness,

O hide the God still more! and make us see
Such as Lucretius drew, a God like Thee.

[4. 483–84]

A few lines later, we catch a glimpse, I think, of a divine form
in the belly of Silenus—one of the Alcibiadean Sileni which
hold "pipes or flutes in their mouths; and . . . are made to
open in the middle . . . and have images of gods inside
them." [50] Pope's Silenus closes more than his snuff box. He
attempts to hide the seams of immanent divinity:

Rous'd at his name, up rose the bowzy Sire,
And shook from out his Pipe the seeds of fire;
Then snapt his box, and strok'd his belly down.

[4. 493–95]

But a chink of light remains. The "Glimpse divine" (4. 652)
is hidden, not destroyed. The effect of the "one dim Ray of
Light" (4. 1), which was "half to shew, half veil the deep

48. *An Essay on Man*, 3 : 284–88. Arthur O. Lovejoy offered useful commentary on this passage in his *Essays in the History of Ideas* (London,
1960), p. 84.

49. In a disparaging comparison with *The Rape of the Lock*, Geoffrey
Tillotson described *The Dunciad* as "the ludicrous, grotesque, lifesize
shadow cast by a piece of an epic poem." *On the Poetry of Pope* (Oxford,
1938), p. 55.

50. "Symposium," sect. 215, in *The Dialogues of Plato*, trans. B. Jowett
(Oxford, 1953), 1 : 547.

Intent" (4. 4), is still felt. *"Religion . . .* veils her sacred fires" (4. 649), she does not extinguish them.

At least a small group of readers have long recognized that *The Dunciad,* in some general way, opposes its own creative verse to the "uncreating word" of Dulness, and that therefore the burden of the poem is far less bleak than the concluding statements might lead us to believe. Now, perhaps, we should realize that the specific opposition is determined and shaped by sacramental form, and that the poem culminates in the transubstantiation of primitive or regressive Nonsense into sacred Sense, in giving body, that is, to God's Word—in extracting the radiant crucifix from the shaggy, satyrlike form of the burlesque.

6

Johnson's "Celestial Wisdom"

Samuel Johnson's *Vanity of Human Wishes* provides a suitable last subject for our study, not only because it is the best poem of the last poet we commonly think of as Augustan, but because it is modeled on a work of Juvenal, an early master in myth-displacing modes, and because that work, the Tenth Satire, is itself modeled on Persius's stoic second satire, which Dryden has analyzed for us as a kind of paradigm of demythology. The three poems in this direct line all have as their subject the vows, prayers, wishes, and ambitions of self-deluded mortals. Dryden's analysis of the essential mechanism employed by Persius is also, I think, a useful description of the procedures of Juvenal and Johnson:

> He shews the original of these vows, and sharply inveighs against them; and . . . not only corrects the false opinion of mankind concerning them, but gives the true doctrine of all addresses made to Heaven.[1]

The key steps, as Dryden observes, are: revealing the source or origin of the mythic assumptions the poet regards as false; and then asserting a new belief or mythic knowledge in its place. Dialectic strives with myth not to destroy it but to subdue it to its original, veracious form.

In the *Vanity of Human Wishes* Juvenal was useful to Johnson in many ways, not least of which was the opportunity

1. *The Poetical Works of John Dryden,* ed. George R. Noyes (Cambridge, Mass., 1950), p. 363.

he offered of invoking a public voice that had become vastly
authoritative. In addition, it is clear that Johnson understood
well the myth-breaking intentions of Juvenal's exempla. Even
when Johnson decided to depart from the Latin text and to
strike out on his own, Juvenal's essential poetic lesson was not
lost on him. That lesson is dramatically set forth in the following passage from Juvenal:

> the things for which we pray, and for which it is [con-
> sidered] right and proper to load the knees of the Gods
> with wax, are either profitless or pernicious! Some men
> are hurled headlong by overgreat power and the envy to
> which it exposes them; they are wrecked by the long and
> illustrious roll of their honours: down come their statues,
> obedient to the rope; the axe hews in pieces their chariot
> wheels and the legs of the unoffending nags. And now the
> flames are hissing, and amid the roar of furnace and of
> bellows the head of the mighty Sejanus, the darling of the
> mob, is burning and crackling, and from that face, which
> was but lately second in the entire world, are being
> fashioned pipkins, basins, frying-pans and slop-pails! [2]
> [ll. 54–64]

The proximity of the phrase *their statues* to the description
of the statues of the gods, encrusted with, and therefore par-
tially formed by, the wax of wish fulfillment, is no accident.
Juvenal's characteristic white heat and splintering anger make
it abundantly clear that the divine images men worship are
only idol-like projections of their own selfish desires. By showing us that statues of such self-worship are no more divine than
the utensils of man's most lowly needs, Juvenal's irony reverses
the myth-arrogating attempts of vain imagination. In much
the same way, Johnson's version of Xerxes's rage for omni-
potence and his biography of the "great man" penetrate
the mythic façade and expose false transference of mythic
power:

2. Quotations from Juvenal's poetry are from *Juvenal and Persius*, trans.
G. G. Ramsay (Cambridge, Mass., 1965).

New pow'rs are claim'd, new pow'rs are still bestow'd,
Till rude resistance lops the spreading god;

[ll. 233–34]

Love ends with hope, the sinking statesman's door
Pours in the morning worshiper no more;

. . . .

For now no more we trace in ev'ry line
Heroic worth, benevolence divine.³

[ll. 79–88]

The reasons for Johnson's substitution of Wolsey for Sejanus
(in many ways the high point of Juvenal's poem) will be
worth our consideration in a moment. Here we should note
that it is to the head of Sejanus's statue that Juvenal particularly calls our attention. It is the head, normally the seat of
reason, but now become falsely mythic and speciously mythifying, which is degraded to the uses and effects of unthinking
appetency. Already at the opening of the poem we are told
that only reason, the dividing or dialectical faculty, can "distinguish true blessings from their opposites, putting aside the
mists of error" (ll. 2–4). Juvenal's dialectical rhetoric operates
with especially merciless incisions on what Plato would have
heartily agreed is a main source of false myth manufacture, the
inflationary rhetoric of vainglorious writers and orators:

It was his genius that cut off the hand, and severed the
neck, of Cicero; never yet did petty pleader stain the
rostra with his blood! *"O happy Fate for the Roman
State / Was the date of my great Consulate!"* Had Cicero
always spoken thus, he might have laughed at the swords
of Antony. [ll. 120–24]

Presumably, Cicero would have been able to keep his head
if he had only had reason enough to check the "overflowing
torrent of his own genius" (l. 119). When we lift the veil of

3. Citations from Johnson's poetry are to volume 6 of *The Yale Edition
of the Works of Samuel Johnson,* ed. E. L. McAdam, Jr. et al. (New
Haven, 1964).

sarcasm we see that the overflowing bad poetry correlates with distortion of reality. Similarly, what strikes Juvenal as dramatically noteworthy in the tragedy of Hannibal is his self-immortalizing textbook exclamations:

> "Nought is accomplished," he cries, "until my Punic host breaks down the city gates, and I plant my standard in the midst of the Subura!" . . . On! on! thou madman, and race over the wintry Alps, that thou mayest be the delight of schoolboys and supply declaimers with a theme!
> [ll. 155–67]

Rhetoric gone mad obscures man's true nature and cripples the exercise of his highest faculty, the reason which allows him to gain the reaches of dignity, truth, and meaningful strength.

Juvenal's grim gaiety subjects Alexander the Great to the same antirhetorical, antimythic treatment. Mere language is shattered. Fevered limbs remain:

> One globe is all too little for the youth of Pella; he chafes uneasily within the narrow limits of the world, as though he were cooped up within the rocks of Gyara or the diminutive Seriphos; but yet when once he shall have entered the city fortified by the potter's art [Babylon], a sarcophagus will suffice him! Death alone proclaims how small are our poor human bodies! [ll. 168–73]

Death not quite alone informs us. The coffinlike syntax of "Unus Pellaeo iuveni non sufficit orbis" (l. 168) itself proclaims that one globe is quite sufficient. Man must see himself in his real dimensions. Reductive appellations like "youth of Pella" or "Ceres' son-in-law" (l. 112) deflate the pride of life and death equally. They make real what was before mythic; and they free the ambience of myth for more worthy objects. Terror inspires men to speak of mere human power in mythic code names: " 'I tremble [says the hanger-on of Tiberius] lest the defeated Ajax should take vengeance for having been so ill-defended.' . . . Such was the talk at the moment about Sejanus" (ll. 84–89). Juvenal's powerfully sane humor stands in marked contrast to the feverish, myth-minting brain of the hanger-on, the severed cranium of self-worshiping Cicero, or the crackling chamber-pot head of idol Sejanus. In the strategy of the poem, Juvenal's humor and irony are the diagnostic reflexes of a healthy mind ruled by an ideal of virtuous reason, a reason of measured expectations and of imaginations shorn of self-deluding vanities, romantic velleities.

Yet we must not misconstrue Juvenal's poetic intention as an attempt to affect a total dispersion of the "mists" with which the poem opens. In another form they are still wafting and curling in the last lines of the poem, where they provide the sustaining atmosphere of the poet's final anagnorisis: "nullum numen habes, si sit prudentia: nos te, / nos facimus, Fortuna, deam caeloque locamus":

> Thou wouldst have no divinity, O Fortune, if we had but wisdom; it is we that make a goddess of thee, and place thee in the skies.
>
> [ll. 365–66]

The "mists of error" have become the shrouds of mystery surrounding *prudentia*. Like all great poet-prophets, Juvenal realized that only a fool or an archenemy of imaginative reason, the instrument of all great human achievement, would wish to annihilate man's sense of the vapor-laden reality that lies beyond his immediate ken or present capacity. Juvenal's poem itself participates in man's need to discover a hidden source. The satire is an exploratory pilgrimage to "the Ganges and the Morn" of man's being (cf. ll. 1–2).

The human mind searches for revelations in "shrines, entrails, and presaging sausages" (cf. l. 355) without realizing that human beings themselves contain an undiscovered cache of knowledge and happiness: the sound mind within a sound body, the unafflicted sanity and prudentia which the reasoned irony of the poem fosters and proclaims to be the real divinity in man. True to the program he set himself in his First Satire, Juvenal here rejects "all the lying tales of Grecian history," with its absurd stories of "how deep rivers failed" (ll. 174 ff.). But, with perfect fidelity to his demythological vision, Juvenal's expedition up the Ganges ends with the reassertion of valuable, humanlike myth in place of the image of god-aspiring excess that currently inhabits man's mythic imagination. "Better than the loves and the banquets and the downy cushions of Sardanapalus," Juvenal tells us, is the heart or mind that "knows neither wrath nor desire" and that can value at its truly heroic rate "the woes and hard labours of Hercules" (ll. 360 ff.)—*Hercules furens* who fought titanically with madness and labored to rechannel deep rivers.

With ample justice critics have repeatedly called our attention to the profound affinity of *The Vanity of Human Wishes* for its announced Juvenalian model.[4] Like Juvenal, Johnson understands that human needs and the desire to pray for their fulfillment are not evil in themselves. He does not ask us to deny the "hunger of imagination" that ravens in all human beings (cf. *Rasselas,* chap. 32). His plea is that we review and revise the objects of hope and fear, while the mythic language he employs ("god," "worshiper," "heroic worth," "benevolence divine") acknowledges the deep-rooted nature of our imaginative constructs or perceptions. As in Juvenal's poem, also, the pieces of the broken myths strewn by early lines are ultimately to be reconstituted into exhortations asserting other myths or beliefs. In both poems the courage of a Xerxes is channeled toward a different commitment.

And yet, though we remind ourselves time and again of the ways in which Juvenal's Stoicism overlaps with Christian doctrine, there is much in Juvenal's poem to challenge the sincere Christian. Juvenal's generals, for example, strive for glory and lose virtue. This is the essential opposition, as Juvenal sees it, no matter who is involved—"be he Greek, Roman, or barbarian" (l. 138). But what if he be Christian? Would not such a man be endangering a good deal more than his Stoic virtue?

4. For discussions of aspects of Johnson's divergence from Juvenal not dealt with here, see Henry Gifford, "The Vanity of Human Wishes," *Review of English Studies,* n.s. 6 (1955): 157–65, and Mary Lascelles, "Johnson and Juvenal," in *New Light on Dr. Johnson,* ed. Frederick W. Hilles (New Haven, 1959), pp. 35–55.

—an infinite amount more? The end of Johnson's poem patiently attempts to fill the damnable vacuum: "petitions yet remain," Johnson adds, "Which heav'n may hear, nor deem religion vain" (ll. 349–50).

But readers like Macaulay have doubted that this is anything more than hasty, extraneous patchwork—Johnson's awkward addendum which falls "decidely short of the sublimity of his Pagan model." [5] From one point of view the reader must ask whether the Christian peroration does, in fact, grow out of the lines that precede it. From another, he cannot help wondering why Johnson, himself so famous in the history of English literature for his passionate refusal to allow the mixing of Christian and pagan elements of poetry, should have decided to pour his deepest Christian feelings into the restrictive mold of a secular Roman satire. In spite of the reverent esteem in which Juvenal's "divine satire" was held by many a devout Christian,[6] the fact remains that the Latin poem is distinctly pagan in outlook and tenet.

To deal with questions and doubts of this kind we must identify the full extent of Johnson's transition to Christian concerns and solutions. For though Johnson reserves his most explicit Christian matter for the de profundis peroration— with its sudden shift from "skies" to "heav'n" and then to "his pow'r" (ll. 348–53)—the soil and bedrock of *The Vanity of Human Wishes,* we must realize, are also Christian in coloration. Almost as if in direct response to Juvenal's purportedly exhaustive survey of military types—Greek, Roman, and barbarian—Johnson carefully couples Alexander the Great with Charles XII of Sweden, and Xerxes with Charles Albert, elector of Bavaria and Holy Roman Emperor. The effect of the conjunction is to suggest that the military man, be he pagan or Christian, is in grave danger of a fall from glory, a fall which is defined in extenso by the overtones of Christian

5. Cited in *The Poems of Samuel Johnson,* ed. D. Nichol Smith and E. L. McAdam, Jr. (Oxford, 1941), p. 47 n.

6. See Ian Jack, *Augustan Satire: Intention and Idiom in English Poetry, 1660–1750* (Oxford, 1966), p. 136.

tragedy. The pairing of Alexander and Charles XII ends with
this description of Charles's fate:

> His fall was destin'd to a barren strand,
> A petty fortress, and a dubious hand;
> He left the name, at which the world grew pale,
> To point a moral, or adorn a tale.
>
> [ll. 219–22]

The difference between this moralizing and Juvenal's shouting
at barbarian Hannibal that he will become "the delight of
schoolboys and supply declaimers with a theme!" is that the
English lines, draped in infernal gloom, hint at a sermonlike,
divine perspective on man's "fall," at the succor of an alterna-
tive Mighty Fortress, and at a contrasting "Name" justly awful
among the nations. These things Charles, and "rapid" (oblivious) Alexander, sorely missed (cf. l. 179).

The poem's movement from "Persia's tyrant to Bavaria's
lord" (l. 224), wends its way to a similar consciousness of the
vanity of this world. Johnson's bent is very much away from
Juvenal's central concern with finding "what will be service-
able for our state" (10.347–48). It was this concern that provided a large part of the logic for Juvenal's preoccupation
with state figures:

> The sides of Democritus shook with unceasing laughter,
> although in the cities of his day there were no purple-
> bordered or purple-striped robes, no fasces, no palanquins,
> no tribunals. What if he had seen the Praetor uplifted in
> his lofty car amid the dust of the Circus, attired in the
> tunic of Jupiter, hitching an embroidered Tyrian toga
> on to his shoulders, and carrying a crown so big that no
> neck could bear the weight of it? [ll. 33–40]

Juvenal deals with the great partly because he espouses an
ideal of larger order that must be sifted through and determined by great men's sanity: the state must find a head and
a crown which are appropriate to each other. Johnson deals

with the great only because they represent an *inflatio ad vanitatem:*

> The bold Bavarian, in a luckless hour,
> Tries the dread summits of Cesarean pow'r,
>
> . . . .
>
> The baffled prince in honour's flatt'ring bloom
> Of hasty greatness finds the fatal doom.
>
> [ll. 241–52]

Here there is a conscious Christian drawing back from what must be rendered unto the emperor and what is also catastrophic temptation to the individual being.

Sejanus's elevation and plummeting are the consequences of whimsy, of mere cruel caprice. He is a passive plaything of fate. His example could not serve the ends of Johnson's poem. Wolsey's "enormous weight" (l. 126) is the effect of his own rearing, the results of his own vast abilities misapplied. His "ruin to the gulphs below" (l. 128) follows from his own free choice to build on weak temporal foundations rather than to depend on the strength of his church and his God. And when Wolsey declines from temporal glory, there is still available to him "the refuge of monastic rest" (l. 118). Here we must remind ourselves of the obvious fact that Johnson chose Wolsey's story because it could imply the Christian belief that spiritual haven is always accessible to fallen man. Johnson's sense of the decorum of his poem (and other factors dealt with below) constrains him not to substitute the special burden of "faith" or "his pow'r" for generalized "fate" until the last breaths of the poem: Wolsey, we hear, built too near the "steeps of fate" (l. 125). Yet there is a pregnant irony in Wolsey's last retrospective sighs, which, even in Christian retreat, can trace his fall to no cause other than the wanting "faith of kings" (l. 120) —in himself! This final neglect or rejection of spiritual haven completes the arc of Wolsey's ruin.

It is typical of the difference between Juvenal's and Johnson's poems that the latter should substitute an excursus on scholarship for Roman concern with oratory. Instead of the Roman schoolboy who prays to Minerva for eloquence and

political fame (cf. 10.114 ff.), we have the young Oxonian who
seeks the fame attendant upon the intercourse of an inspired
mind with the secrets of God's creation—the mind of a Lydiat
or Galileo:

> When first the college rolls receive his name,
> The young enthusiast quits his ease for fame;
> Through all his veins the fever of renown
> Burns from the strong contagion of the gown;
> O'er Bodley's dome his future labours spread,
> And Bacon's mansion trembles o'er his head.
> Are these thy views? proceed, illustrious youth,
> And virtue guard thee to the throne of Truth!
>
> [ll. 135–42]

The prayer of the "young enthusiast" is determined by a belief in a god within and in an enthroned Truth, which are in
turn conditioned by the special nature of the Christian schol-
arly heritage, by a gown half-academic, half-ecclesiastical, by
the reverent precincts of Friar Bacon's or Bodley's palace of
wisdom. Reason's "brightest ray" is by itself insufficient to
make the scholar "wise" (cf. ll. 145–58). Another ingredient is
required.

By this time we have realized that the cores of Juvenal's
Tenth Satire and Johnson's *Vanity of Human Wishes* differ
substantially. In spite of Johnson's dramatic, interminable
struggle to retain mere sanity and mere life—a sound mind
even in a body racked with pain—we must not be misled into
a too easy identification of Johnson's theme with Juvenal's
ratio or *prudentia*. Juvenal's poem was invaluable to Johnson
as a paragon of reason's war against false myth and of ratiocinative poetry's reenstatement of virtuous reason as man's
divinelike faculty. Johnson's imitation enabled him to participate in Juvenal's proclamation of prudentia. But then
Johnson, in turn, in his own controlled form of the Brutus-
crisis, radically altered the centrality of his master's teaching
and labored to reduce to a part that which for Juvenal was
the framework of the whole—the healthful mind, reason's
brightest ray.

In characteristic Johnsonian fashion, *The Vanity of Human Wishes* penetrates to the mainspring of the mode it was employing. Johnson emphasizes the workings of the imagination itself. At the outset he tells us that he would show "how hope and fear, desire and hate, / O'erspread with snares the clouded maze of fate" (ll. 5–6). His long series of exempla reaches its climax in the question, "Where then shall Hope and Fear their objects find?" (l. 343). Walter Jackson Bate has remarked that a central concern of the poem is to show that, "in the very activity or process of wishing, there are inherent liabilities that are able to undercut the wish itself," especially that the "capacity of the imagination" always exceeds "actual enjoyment." [7] In *The Vanity of Human Wishes,* Johnson focuses on the myth-creating faculty itself, the human imagination, and then redirects it to find new objects. He offers a model of myth revision in which his encounter with Juvenal is itself at the heart of the effort to revise the objects of imagination. In fact, the most poignantly dramatic aspect of *The Vanity of Human Wishes* is the poet's wrestling with his angel Juvenal. He did not fight unaided.

We have seen that Johnson's poem is subtly pervaded by the Christian idea of man's fall. Desire for "hasty greatness" causes men to reach for "honour's flatt'ring bloom" which, once plucked, brings with it the inevitable "fatal doom" (ll. 251–52). Their stories are matter for a repeating "tale" of fall. We should not be surprised to find that when Johnson came to write his Christian version of Juvenal's poem—a version not less but more heroic than any Stoic, tragic satire—his imagination should have turned automatically to a poem that contains the central demythological proclamation of fall and redemption in English literature. In fact, he chose a poem which was itself a Christian version of the most estimable Greek and Roman poetic form, and which, according to Johnson, "considered with respect to design, may claim the first place, and with respect to performance the second, among the produc-

---

7. *The Achievement of Samuel Johnson* (New York, 1955), pp. 81–82.

tions of the human mind." [8] The deepest meaning of *The Vanity of Human Wishes,* avowedly an imitation of a pagan poem, depends upon the intimation of the displacing myth of *Paradise Lost.*

For two centuries, critics—great poets among them—have caviled at the seemingly egregious redundancy of Johnson's opening lines:

> Let observation with extensive view,
> Survey mankind, from China to Peru;
> Remark each anxious toil, each eager strife,
> And watch the busy scenes of crouded life.

Tennyson summed up a whole tradition of amused impatience with these lines by asking why Johnson did not write, more simply, "Let observation, with extended observation, observe extensively." [9] We, too, may wonder what Johnson imagined his intensive repetition might accomplish, until we recognize that his opening lines represent a bold departure from the empirical perspective of Juvenal's poem and that they are, in fact, a rehearsal of the introduction to the Pisgah-sight offered to fallen man in the eleventh and twelfth books of *Paradise Lost* —the very same Miltonic view Pope had recently invoked in *The Dunciad* (3. 61 ff.). It is here that solitary man gets his first glimpses of busy scenes and crowded life. Milton tells us that Michael and Adam ascend the hill of Paradise to see the earth in "clearest Ken" and "amplest reach of prospect," and that their view was not less extensive than the temptation to vanity offered Christ by Satan in the wilderness, a sight of vanity from China to Peru (cf. 11. 385 ff.):

> His Eye might there command wherever stood
> City of old or modern Fame, the Seat

8. *Lives of the English Poets,* ed. George Birkbeck Hill (Oxford, 1905), 1 : 170.

9. Cited, together with similar opinions attributed to Coleridge and Wordsworth, in *Poems of Samuel Johnson,* ed. Smith and McAdam, p. 30 n. In the same place, notice is taken of the use of the phrase "from China to Peru" in the conclusion of Sir William Temple's *Of Poetry* (1690).

Of mightiest Empire, from the destin'd Walls
Of *Cambalu,* seat of *Cathaian Can.*

And he might have seen, "in Spirit,"

Cusco in *Peru,* the richer seat
Of *Atabalipa,* and yet unspoil'd
Guiana, whose great City *Geryon*'s Sons
Call *El Dorado:* but to nobler sights
Michael from *Adam's* eyes the Film remov'd
Which that false Fruit that promis'd clearer sight
Had bred; then purg'd with Euphrasy and Rue
The visual Nerve, for he had much to see.

Johnson opens with a plea, already almost a prayer, for truly
unobstructed vision, for extensive view, which is by no means
automatically available to a creature whose eyes have been
rendered opaque by spiritual fall. He superimposes on Juvenal's survey both a rejection of the Satan-like temptation to
vanity, which the world persistently holds out to the sincere
Christian, and a painful preview of the sorrowful plight of the
fallen children of fallen Adam.[10]

The blending of Milton with Juvenal was not hard to en-
vision. Aside from the fact, already illustrated, that both poets
were profoundly demythological, both the Tenth Satire and
Paradise Lost, particularly in Michael's hard words of comfort, sprang from a good deal of common soil. Michael's advice, for example,

Nor love thy Life, nor hate; but what thou liv'st
Live well, how long or short permit to Heav'n,

[11. 553–54]

sounds as though it might be a quotation from the Tenth
Satire because it echoes the same pronouncements of Horace,
Seneca, and Martial that stand behind Juvenal's counsel. The
contours of Juvenal's and Milton's surveys coincide in ways

10. For a useful defense of Johnson's opening couplet on other grounds,
see Arieh Sachs, *Passionate Intelligence: Imagination and Reason in the
Work of Samuel Johnson* (Baltimore, 1967), pp. 77–79.

that permitted a decorous allusive overlay of Miltonic, Christian counterheroic upon Juvenalian counterheroic. Juvenal's observation, for instance, that

> full oft has a land been destroyed by the vainglory of a few, by the lust for honour and for a title that shall cling to the stones that guard their ashes
>
> [ll. 142–44]

and Milton's disgust at those

> styl'd great Conquerors,
> Patrons of Mankind, Gods, and Sons of Gods,
> Destroyers rightlier call'd and Plagues of men,
>
> [11. 695–97]

both have their places in Johnson's Christian revulsion at the idolatrous glory for which

> in distant lands the Britons shine,
> And stain with blood the Danube or the Rhine;
> . . . .
> . . . Reason frowns on War's unequal game,
> Where wasted nations raise a single name.
>
> [ll. 181–86]

A similar mixture is to be found in Johnson's description of Xerxes as a false god and a disease or growth, a "spreading god," who must be excised. Juvenal's argument forms the skeleton and flesh of Johnson's poem while the marrow and lifeblood—the powerful sense of man's fallen condition, the conception of the world as temptation to vanity, and the heartfelt need to transcend mere rationalism—are Miltonic. Johnson's frowning reason depends on a store of wisdom and vision no Adam can achieve completely without a Michael, no reader without a truly Christian poet; for reason of this kind is the effect of transmutation, both of capacities within and of experience without, which cannot be compassed alone. When you pray, says Johnson,

> Pour forth thy fervours for a healthful mind,
> Obedient passions, and a will resign'd;

For love, which scarce collective man can fill;
For patience sov'reign o'er transmuted ill;
For faith, that panting for a happier seat,
Counts death kind Nature's signal of retreat:
. . . .
With these celestial wisdom calms the mind,
And makes the happiness she does not find.

[ll. 359–68]

Such heavenly wisdom can be achieved only in the pellucid
interval between man's ascent to and descent from vision. This
is the vision of human experience, which is itself life-changing
experience even if it is only poetic or visionary experience, because it is communicated by a poet whose own fervid prayers
are momentarily being answered. Just as in Juvenal's poem
the use of prudentia, manifested in reasoned irony, itself fosters prudentia and proclaims it to be the true gift of the gods,
so Johnson's faith-filled "celestial wisdom" manifests itself in
a grace-gifted retreat to a mount of true sermon.[11] It is a sermon that moves the poem toward a redemption of the spec-
tacle of fallen man. Johnson's anagnorisis, his salvaging of the
substance of Juvenal's defective reason, seems purposefully
constructed from materials very like Adam's first and last prophetic moments. As Adam and Michael climb the holy hill,
Adam already sees that ill must somehow be painfully transmuted:

Ascend, I follow thee, safe Guide, the path
Thou lead'st me, and to the hand of Heav'n submit,
However chast'ning, to the evil turn
My obvious breast, arming to overcome
By suffering, and earn rest from labor won,
If so I may attain.

[11. 371–76]

By the end of the vision, Michael has shown Adam that life
has been fashioned so that he may indeed "attain" these internal goods; in Johnson's words,

11. Ian Jack, *Augustan Satire*, p. 138, remarks that "Johnson is in the
pulpit throughout, addressing a congregation."

These goods for man the laws of heav'n ordain,
These goods he grants, who grants the pow'r to gain.

[ll. 365–66]

In the moment just before they descend, Adam confirms that
he has learned his difficult lesson,

> that to obey is best,
> And love with fear the only God, to walk
> As in his presence, ever to observe
> His providence, and on him sole depend,
> Merciful over all his works, with good
> Still overcoming evil . . .
>
> . . . .
> Taught this by his example whom I now
> Acknowledge my Redeemer ever blest.

[12. 561–73]

To which Michael replies in words and accents that were difficult for someone like Johnson, intent on "celestial widsom," to
forget:

> This having learnt, thou hast attain'd the sum
> Of wisdom; hope no higher . . .
>
> . . . .
> . . . only add
> Deeds to thy knowledge answerable, add Faith,
> Add Virtue, Patience, Temperance, add Love,
> By name to come call'd Charity, the soul
> Of all the rest: then wilt thou not be loath
> To leave this Paradise, but shalt possess
> A paradise within thee, happier far.

[12. 575–87]

Johnson's "happier seat" or "happiness" and Milton's "paradise . . . happier far" are not very different. Both are made
in the mind or soul, and both, in the poems themselves, are
the effects of transmutation—of Hesperian gardens in Milton's
case, or, in Johnson's of Roman half-wisdom that yields divine
truth. Johnson's piercing muse is a version of Democritus, the
Silenic figure whose shaking sides open to reveal tragic truth.

Johnson's Democritus is of a more sorrowful cast than Juvenal's, whose gaiety is externally balanced (though never
really counterweighted) by a weeping Heraclitus. Johnson's
muse includes the moist-eyed philosopher as well as the divinity who sojourns in the vale of tears. Johnson's muse, like Milton's, fulfills herself in the decisive denouncement or proclamation that issues from the demythological sermon: it is the
paradise of man, the place of spirit, which has in all ages given
life to the idea of civilized existence. It is the salvation that
"shall be Preacht . . . to the Sons / Of . . . Faith wherever
through the world." This is the comforter sent to restore the
covenant, the bond of true conviction; this is the indwelling
spirit.

Index

Abdiel, 75

Abraham, 39, 49, 50, 52, 73, 77, 78, 133

Absalom, 89, 92, 95, 101, 102

Achilles, 63, 64

Achitophel, 92–97 passim, 101, 103

Adam, 58, 59, 60, 67, 71, 72, 73, 76, 99, 100, 101, 106, 117, 118, 167, 168, 169, 170, 171

Adonis, 68

Adriel, 88, 95

Aemilianus, 31. *See* Scipio

Aeneas, 30, 63, 67

Agamemnon, 34

Ajax, 159

Alcibiades. *See* Silenus Alcibiadis

Alexander the Great, 159, 162, 163. *See also* Ammon

Allen, Don Cameron, 62, 62*n*, 65, 65*n*, 116*n*, 140*n*

Amiel, 87

Amiot, François, 149*n*

Ammon, 128. *See* Alexander the Great

Anderson, W. S., 19, 20

Anne (queen), 112, 113, 119, 121, 124

Antichrist, 132, 140. *See also* Mock Mass

Antony, 158

Apis, 32, 66

Apollo, 27

Arthurian legend, 62

Astarte, 67

Atabalipa (Atahuallpa), 168

Atlas, 48, 53

Augustus (emperor of Rome), 1, 2, 3, 21–27 passim, 126, 128

Bacon, Roger, 165

Barzillai, 87, 90

Bate, Walter Jackson, 166

Belinda, 124, 144

Bentley, Richard, 134, 143

Bethel, Slingsby, 106

Black Mass. *See* Mock Mass

Bladen, Thomas, 145

Blake, William, 80, 99

Bodkin, Maud, 67*n*

Boileau, Nicholas Despréaux, 129

Bolingbroke. *See* St. John, Henry

Bowra, C. M., 63*n*

Boyle, Robert, 85

Brinton, Crane, xii*n*

Brower, Reuben, 1, 1*n*, 4, 41, 125*n*

Bubo, 126

Bultmann, Rudolf, 5, 6

Busiris, 70

Calvin, John, 39, 77, 78

Caroline (queen), 127

Casaubon, Isaac, 18

Cassirer, Ernst, xi, xii, xiii, 7

Castor, 25, 27

Catiline, 34

Cecropid, 32

Ceres, 65, 118, 119, 159

Cethegus, 34

Chancellor, E. Beresford, 147*n*

Charles Albert (elector of Bavaria), 162

Charles II, 83, 88, 94, 112